Wartime Recipes

FROM THE MARITIMES

1939

D1215694

Devonna Edwards

NIMBUS
PUBLISHING

*This book is dedicated to the memory of my father-in-law,
William Edwards (at left), and his brothers, Daniel and
Harry, all of whom fought in World War Two.*

Nimbus Publishing Limited
PO Box 9166, Halifax, NS   B3K 5M8
(902) 455-4286

Design: Gwen North
Cover design: Heather Bryan
Printed and bound in Canada

Canadian Cataloguing in Publication Data
Edwards, Devonna
        Wartime Recipes from the Maritimes, 1939-1943
        Includes index.
        ISBN 1-55109-337-5

1. Cookery—Maritime Provinces—History—20th century. I. Title.
TX715.6.E39 2001   641.5'09715'09044   C2001-900101-0

Canadä   The Canada Council | Le Conseil des Arts
             for the Arts | du Canada

We acknowledge the financial support of the Government of Canada through the Book Publishing Industry Development Program (BPIDP) and the Canada Council for our publishing activities.

Table of Contents

Acknowledgements

My husband calls me "a history junkie," and it's true that there is nothing I like more than to scour old newspapers to see how people lived in bygone days. It was during one of my many trips to the public archives in Halifax during the summer of 1992 that I came up with the idea of collecting wartime recipes. What people ate and cooked tell us much about how they lived; contemporary newspaper food columns, advertisements, and articles offer a wealth of information about how rationing during World War Two affected home-front consumers in the Maritimes.

Some of the recipes will seem downright peculiar to today's reader, but many of them will be appreciated by anyone who likes to cook tasty and nutritious meals without blowing the grocery budget. The recipes have been formatted so that they are easy to follow. (I hate recipes that neglect to inform you until it's too late that the eggs should have been separated, or that the oven needs to be preheated!) Some of them have been adapted to suit modern tastes—substituting oil for lard, for example—while others have not been touched, and are best left for the amusement of the armchair cook!

I'd like to thank my husband Donnie, my sons Donald Jr. and Darcy, and also my mother Mary O'Brien, who have always encouraged my interest in things past. My late father, John O'Brien, served in the war and has a very special place in my heart. Thanks also to *The Halifax Mail Star*, Antigonish's *The Casket*, and the helpful staff at Nova Scotia Archives and Records Management.

You Say You Want to Help?

"YOU SAY YOU WANT TO HELP … Not all of us can shoulder a gun or pilot a bomber … but we can all help win this war, and speed the day of Victory." The message was clear. Canadian women were being called to take up arms and join in the battle against Hitler. But this was no recruitment poster for the R.C.A.F., the Wrens, or the Canadian Women's Army Corps. This was an appeal to housewives, young and old, to "fight the good fight" in their homes and kitchens: to avoid unnecessary buying; to refuse to hoard; to conserve fuel and electricity; to "get in the scrap" and recycle everything from cookware to kitchen scraps; and, above all, to feed their families well to keep them fighting fit.

World War Two forever transformed the lives of Canadian women. Aside from the personal life changes brought about by the loss of husbands, sons, fathers, and brothers to the battlefield, women entered the workforce in unprecedented numbers. Donning trousers and overalls, thousands of women took over traditionally male jobs in factories, shipyards, lumber mills, and coal mines. They put on ties and entered corporate offices and government institutions. Thousands entered active service, driving ambulances and trucks, flying planes, and working in hospitals. And countless numbers of women provided volunteer services, both on their own initiative and through organizations such as the Red Cross. However, it was the housewives in particular who were encouraged by wartime propaganda to act as soldiers on the "kitchen front."

Domestic battles on the home front were fought in the midst of rationing and shortages. Compared to the privations suffered by civilians in Europe, these were more of an inconvenience than a real hardship. But home-front rationing was vital to the war effort; it not only aided hunger and unrest in Europe but it also controlled domestic food prices and ensured fair distribution of goods. And rationing enabled Canadian civilians—women in particular—to contribute in a meaningful way to the war effort.

Wartime rationing was initiated in order to free up consumer goods for military use and distribution to allied countries overseas. It was also a vital way of limiting the consumption of those commodities that had to be imported into Canada, since merchant shipping cut into naval reserves as well as put lives at risk. While the rationing of certain foods such as coffee, tea, sugar, butter, and meat had a direct impact on what people cooked and ate on the home front, the demand for materials such as metals, fuels, plastics, and rubber affected wartime kitchens both directly and indirectly. Gasoline was rationed, creating difficulties in transporting even non-rationed foods such as eggs, which caused shortages and high prices. Coal and wood were at a premium, which had implications for commercial food industries as well as home consumers. Rubber, plastics, fats, and metals were desperately needed for wartime machinery and weapons, which meant that this was not the time for housewives to be splurging on matched sets of cookware or commercially canned fruits and vegetables.

"Re-use" and "recycle," words that have come back into fashion in our consumer society, were the catchwords of the day. Canada's furnaces, foundries, and mills were thundering at top-speed to produce steel for ships, tanks, guns, planes, and munitions. The war effort needed every available piece of scrap metal, from brass beds to heavy aluminum and iron pots, which patriotic housewives exchanged for lightweight aluminum cookware. People even saved their empty toothpaste and shaving-cream tubes, which in Nova Scotia alone added up to over 1,500 pounds of tin. Newsprint and paper of all kinds were recycled and put to use in wrapping detonation charges, casing parachute flare charges, and making cartridge wadding. Paperboard cartons made of waste paper were vital for packing materials shipped overseas. And fat and bones were needed to make glycerin and glue for weapons and airplanes.

Housewives and schoolchildren headed salvage drives to collect these important waste products. And there were other ways in which women were encouraged to contribute to victory. Grocery stores sponsored newspaper ads with headlines such as "Early-Week Shopping Helps War Effort," urging women to be patriotic and avoid weekend shopping, which created "bottlenecks" and prevented store employees from participating in important war services. Women were also charged with the responsibility of keeping their families well fed and "fighting fit," despite rationing and food shortages. This meant that housewives had to be imaginative in meal planning and economical in the kitchen. The Great Depression had already trained a generation of resourceful housewives, but the wartime call for patriotism added another dimension to domestic thrift. Women were expected to economize in the kitchen and spend their savings on Victory Bonds and War Savings Certificates, which they did in great measure. Between January 1940 and the end of the war, Canadians poured 8.8 billion dollars into these savings programs.

The need for economy meant that nothing was wasted. As one wartime advertisement for Savings Stamps illustrated, the patriotic housewife "christened [her] garbage can 'Hitler' and … he doesn't get anything that's worth anything." Not wasting food translated into thinking up imaginative, if not always palatable, ways to use leftovers. Cookery columnists suggested all sorts of ideas to "give leftovers new appeal," which meant that the ubiquitous croquette, moulded gelatin salads, or simply "hash" were served up in many kitchens. Fortunately for the housewife, children also received instructions in patriotic behaviour, which usually boiled down to eating what was put in front of them without complaint: "I tell my children that as long as Jack is overseas, we'll eat hash and like it!"

While women were urged to serve their country in the kitchen by feeding their families nutritious and economical meals, they were also warned against the dangers of hoarding. The Department of National War Service issued posters threatening, "You need not hoard. You must not hoard. YOU MUST OBEY THE LAW." Certain rationed foods, such as sugar, were under strict regulations. It was illegal to have on hand more than two weeks worth of sugar at any given time. However, especially at the beginning of the war, people were uncertain how to use their ration books, and they frequently stocked up on supplies as soon as their coupons became valid. This resulted in reduced stocks and the rapid emptying of store shelves.

The ration books themselves were distributed by the Wartime Prices and Trade Board in Ottawa to over 600 Local Ration Boards that served "every city, town, and hamlet" in Canada. The 75,000 Canadians who lived in remote areas such as the Yukon and the Northwest Territories were exempt from rationing. For the rest, newspapers informed them when and where to pick up their ration books, which could not be sent through the mail. The small, passport-sized books contained pages of coloured stamps or coupons, each colour representing a rationed item— red for sugar and green for tea and coffee, for example. The coupons had to be detached in the presence of a storekeeper; it was illegal for anyone to accept loose coupons. Each individual was issued a serial number, and had to enter his or her name and address in ink on the detachable postcard, which had to be returned when applying for a new ration book. Losing a postcard or using it "improperly" resulted in complications and delays. The consequences of forgetting to collect the bi-monthly ration book were equally frustrating, as 18,000 Haligonians learned in March 1943 when miscommunications and bad weather resulted in large numbers losing out on two weeks worth of sugar, tea, coffee, and butter.

Ration books were the housewife's primary weapon on the domestic front, where she waged war against waste, hoarding, poor nutrition, and low morale with the same sense of urgency as the generals who mapped out battle campaigns in Europe. After all, as the popular slogan cautioned fussy eaters, it was better to have "Potluck with Churchill today than Humble Pie under Hitler tomorrow."

Guns Instead of Butter!

Butter, Eggs, and Cheese

BUTTER is four Pats a Week in Britain

HITLER chose "Guns instead of butter." So the Nazis have guns! We must catch up . . . and beat them.

They tortured people to make them save.

We must save willingly.

So it's up to us, each one of us, to economize of our own free will . . . to economize and buy War Savings Stamps so that we can outstrip our enemies with planes and tanks and guns and ships . . . so that our soldiers may be better equipped than the enemy they have to conquer.

Women must help by economizing in the kitchen, by patching and darning, by shopping carefully and cutting out waste. Make up your mind now to buy one, two, five or more War Savings Stamps *every week*. You can. You must!

Buy War Savings Stamps from banks, post offices, telephone offices, department stores, druggists, grocers, tobacconists, book stores and other retail stores.

National War Finance Committee

Guns Instead of Butter!

In one of its many campaigns to encourage women to economize in the kitchen and buy War Savings Stamps, the National War Finance Committee pointed out that Hitler chose "guns instead of butter"—and so must the Canadian housewife. In fact, glycerin, used in high explosives, was made from fat, and so not only was butter rationed during the war, but Canadians were urged to "get in the scrap" and save their fat drippings, which they collected in recycled tin cans. The government called for 40 million pounds of fat for the war effort, and children as well as adults participated in fat salvage drives. In March 1942, movie theatres in Halifax and Dartmouth offered students free admission in exchange for salvaged fats.

During the early days of rationing, people often went "butterless" for days on end. Not knowing when their next ration coupons would become valid, shoppers would stock up when butter became available. This caused occasional "rushes" on butter at grocery stores, despite official warnings against "panic buying" and hoarding.

Ironically, margarine was not an option for wartime Canadians, because dairy farmers lobbied successfully to keep it banned until the late 1940s, when the Canadian Women's Institute finally convinced the government to allow its sale and manufacture. (Even then it was bleached white to distinguish it from butter, and sold with "colour buds" that could be kneaded in before using.) And although people were encouraged to substitute drippings from bacon and other fatty meats for butter or shortening, recipes such as "Wartime Butter" and "Butter Stretcher" also became very popular. These were variations on the same theme: blending butter with shortening, cream or "top milk," and either eggs or gelatin. Such recipes usually called for a liberal amount of salt to improve (or hide!) the flavour, and the addition of yellow food colouring to "overcome the objectionable lardy" appearance.

While the British housewife had to rely on powdered eggs during the war, fresh eggs were not rationed in the Maritimes. However, because of labour shortages and gasoline rationing, eggs were often in short supply in urban areas. Women soon learned how to stretch a few eggs to feed many mouths, and pancakes were a popular dish at breakfast and other meals. Because butter and other fats were too precious to waste in the frying pan, wartime cooks often used the trick of rubbing a raw potato over the bottom of the pan.

The war also affected the availability of cheese. Prior to the war, Canadians were used to buying fine imported cheeses from Europe. The outbreak of war put an abrupt halt to the European export market, and what stocks were in reserve became expensive and hard to find. The shortage of cheese, however, prompted the development of Quebec's cheese industry, and Canadian Cheddar is now considered one of the finest in the world.

Plain Pancakes

Makes 10–12

The key to successful pancakes is to have the pan hot enough that a sprinkling of water sizzles. Don't turn the pancakes until they have set and the bubbles on the exposed surface break. Half a finely chopped apple added to the batter makes a nice variation.

2 cups flour	2 eggs
2 teaspoons sugar	1 1/2 cups milk
3 teaspoons baking powder	1 tablespoon melted fat
1/2 teaspoon salt	

Sift together the dry ingredients in a large bowl. Beat the eggs and milk together in a separate bowl, then stir quickly into the dry mixture. Stir in the melted fat. Pour from a pitcher onto a hot griddle or lightly greased frying pan. Cook until bubbles form on the top, and edges begin to lift. Turn and cook on the other side. Keep pancakes warm while you make the rest, then serve at once.

Potato Pancakes

Serves 4

Six medium-sized potatoes will produce two cups of grated potato. Unless you're determined to make these in wartime style, use a food processor or food chopper to speed up the process!

2 cups grated raw potatoes	1 tablespoon fine fresh
1 egg, beaten	breadcrumbs
	1 1/2 teaspoons salt

Combine the grated potatoes with the beaten egg, breadcrumbs, and salt. Mix well. Form into patties, using your hands, and place in a hot, lightly greased frying pan. Flatten the pancakes with a spatula, and turn them over when browned underneath. Cook until crisp and browned on both sides.

Crumb Pancakes

Makes 12–15

1/2 cup flour	2 eggs
3 teaspoons baking powder	1 1/2 cups milk
1/2 teaspoon salt	2 tablespoons melted fat
1 1/2 cups fine dry breadcrumbs	

Sift the flour, baking powder, and salt in a large bowl. Stir in the breadcrumbs. Beat the eggs and milk in a separate bowl, and stir into the dry ingredients. Stir in the melted fat. Pour from a pitcher onto a hot griddle or lightly greased frying pan. Cook until bubbles form on the top, and the edges begin to lift. Turn and cook on the other side. Keep pancakes warm while you make the rest, then serve at once.

Victory Garden Pancakes

Makes 12

If you save the juices from the grated onion and potatoes, you can use them to moisten the batter, adding less milk. Serve these pancakes with a tomato or cheese sauce for a simple and nutritious meal.

1 cup flour	2 potatoes, finely grated
1 1/2 teaspoons baking powder	2 cups spinach or other leafy green, finely shredded
1 1/2 teaspoons salt	1/2 head leaf lettuce, finely shredded
2 eggs, beaten	oil, for frying
1/2 cup milk	
1 small onion, finely grated	

Sift together the dry ingredients in a large bowl. Beat the eggs and milk together in a separate bowl, then stir quickly into the dry mixture. Fold in the prepared vegetables. Drop the batter by spoonfuls onto a hot, greased frying pan. Cook on both sides until browned.

Fluffy Omelet

Serves 4

This recipe was submitted to The Halifax Mail *by Frances H. Watts of Collingwood Corner, NS. Given wartime fuel and wood shortages, frying the omelet slowly on the stovetop and then finishing it off in the oven would have been considered a bit wasteful.*

2 tablespoons minute tapioca	1 tablespoon melted butter
3/4 cup scalded milk	salt and pepper
4 eggs, separated	

Preheat the oven to 300°F. Combine the tapioca and milk in the top of a double boiler. Bring to a simmer and cook for 10 minutes. Season with salt and pepper. Meanwhile, beat the egg yolks until creamy and pale. In a separate bowl, whisk the whites until stiff but not dry. Stir the butter and egg yolks into the milk. Remove from heat and fold in the beaten egg whites. Pour the mixture into a hot, greased frying pan, then reduce the heat and cook for 15 minutes. Place the pan in the oven for 4 minutes to cook the top of the omelet. Fold the omelet in the pan and serve at once.

Orange Waffles

Makes 6–12

Serve with orange marmalade or blueberry syrup.

2 cups sifted cake flour	1 1/2 teaspoons grated
1/4 cup sugar	orange zest
2 teaspoons baking powder	2/3 cup milk
1/2 teaspoon salt	6 tablespoons melted butter
2 eggs, separated	

Sift together the dry ingredients in a large bowl. Beat the egg yolks with the orange zest, milk, and melted butter. Stir into the dry ingredients, just until smooth. In a separate bowl, whisk the egg whites until stiff but not dry, and fold into the batter. Cook in batches in a preheated waffle iron.

Pineapple Waffles

Makes 8–10

1 3/4 cups flour	2 eggs
1 tablespoon sugar	3/4 cup milk
3 teaspoons baking powder	1/2–3/4 cup crushed and
1/2 teaspoon salt	drained canned pineapple

Sift together the dry ingredients in a large bowl. Beat the eggs with the milk, then stir into the dry ingredients. Fold the pineapple into the batter and bake in batches in a preheated waffle iron.

Baked Eggs in Rolls

Serves 4

2 tablespoons soft butter	4 eggs
1/2 teaspoon dry mustard	salt, pepper, and paprika
4 round bread rolls	chopped parsley, to garnish

Preheat the oven to 300°F and grease a pie plate. Blend the butter and mustard together. Cut the tops off the rolls and hollow out the soft centres. Spread the seasoned butter all over the rolls, inside and out. Place the rolls in the pie plate. Break an egg into each hollow and sprinkle with salt, pepper, and paprika. Bake for 15 minutes, until the eggs are cooked. Garnish with parsley and serve at once.

Mushroom Scrambled Eggs

Serves 4

Canned soups went a long way in stretching a meal.

1/2 cup canned mushroom soup	4 eggs
1/4 cup warm water	salt and pepper

Blend the mushroom soup with the warm water in a medium-sized bowl. Beat in the eggs until light. Season with salt and pepper and cook in a greased frying pan.

Baked Eggs au Gratin

Serves 4

5 tablespoons milk	1/2 cup grated cheese
2 cups fresh bread cubes	4 eggs
salt and pepper	

Preheat the oven to 350°F and grease a baking dish. Combine the milk and bread in a bowl and season with salt and pepper. Place in the prepared baking dish, and sprinkle with cheese. Gently break the eggs over top. Bake for 15 minutes, until set.

Eggs in Cracker Nests

Serves 4

4 tablespoons grated cheese	4 eggs
2 teaspoons water	salt and pepper
24 crackers, crumbled	

Preheat the oven to 350°F and grease a 4-cup muffin pan. Melt the cheese in the top of a double boiler, stirring in the water and cracker crumbs. Divide the mixture between the muffin cups, pressing it in firmly to create "nests." Break an egg into each nest, season with salt and pepper, and bake for 15 minutes.

Eggs and Onions

Serves 6

2 cups white sauce
12 small onions, peeled and
   sliced
8 slices of bacon, chopped
   and fried until crisp

6 hardboiled eggs, sliced
1/2 cup buttered
   breadcrumbs

Preheat the oven to 350°F and grease a baking dish. Pour half the white sauce into the baking dish and add half the onions. Scatter the fried bacon bits on top, followed by half the sliced eggs. Repeat the layers of white sauce, onions, and eggs, sprinkle with the breadcrumbs, and bake for 1 1/4 hours.

Spicy Eggs

Serves 6

1 cup milk
1 bay leaf
5 eggs, beaten
1/4 teaspoon curry powder

1/4 teaspoon salt
1 cup fresh breadcrumbs
6 slices buttered toast, to
   serve

Heat the milk with the bay leaf in the top of a double boiler. Remove the bay leaf, beat in the eggs and seasoning, and stir in the bread-crumbs. Cook slowly, stirring frequently, until the eggs are set.
Serve on buttered toast.

Two Pounds per Week

Meat and Poultry

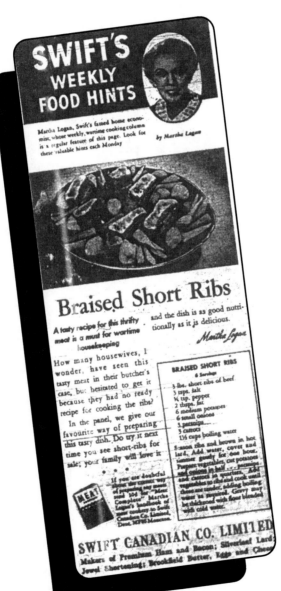

Two Pounds per Week

In 1942 the Wartime Trade and Prices Board set weekly meat rations at two pounds per person. Even to a generation of "meat and two veg" cooks, meat rationing was more of a nuisance than a deprivation. But when every ounce of meat had its price in ration coupons, meal planning became an art for both butchers and customers. Restaurants featured "meatless" Tuesdays and Thursdays, and housewives calculated how to make Sunday's roast last well into the following week. Canadians were spurred on by reminders of how their allied citizens in Europe dined. Headlines such as "The Average Canadian Literally Eats a Meal Fit for a King" reported that meat was "seldom served in the palace more than once a week."

Halifax newspaper advertisements from the period indicate that cheaper cuts of meat, including blade roasts, short rib roasts, and rump roasts, were more frequently available than prime cuts. Corned beef and "Hamburg steak—freshly minced" were also commonly advertised. The latter was equivalent to what we know as ground beef (although housewives often minced their own), and, promoted as "delicious in timbales, loaves, soufflés, croquettes, or hash," it became very popular in wartime kitchens. When supplemented by breadcrumbs, cereal, or pastry, ground meat, like eggs, could be stretched to feed many mouths. Variety meats such as liver and kidneys were not rationed, and women were encouraged not to shy away from these "flavourful and nutritious" sources of protein.

New England Boiled Dinner

Serves 6–8

Cured and salted meats remained popular even after refrigeration made possible the transportation of fresh meats. "Corned" beef refers to the corn-sized salt crystals used to brine, or cure, the meat. This recipe probably travelled north with New England loyalists, and is still a popular Maritime dish during the cold winter months.

2 pounds corned beef brisket
1/2 tablespoon peppercorns
1 bay leaf
1 small head of young
    cabbage, cut in wedges
3 turnips, peeled and
    chopped

6 carrots, peeled and chopped
6 potatoes, peeled and
    chopped
6 small beets

Place the beef in a pot and cover with cold water. Bring to a simmer over medium heat, and remove the surface scum using a slotted spoon. Add the peppercorns and bay leaf. Reduce the heat, cover, and simmer for 1 1/2–2 hours, until very tender. Remove from the pot and keep warm. Add the cabbage, turnips, carrots, and potatoes to the pot. Bring to a simmer and cook for 30 minutes. Cook the beets separately in salted boiling water, until tender. Drain, peel, and quarter. Slice the beef and serve it on a large platter, surrounded by the cooked vegetables.

Beef Pot Roast with Dressing

Serves 8

3 tablespoons fat	1 egg
4-pound chuck or rump roast	3/4 cup milk
1 large onion, sliced finely	4 cups buttered breadcrumbs
1/2 cup water	1 teaspoon poultry seasoning
3 potatoes, peeled and cubed	salt and pepper
1 cup canned tomatoes	

Heat the fat in a casserole and sear the roast on all sides. Stir in the onion and cook for 5 minutes. Add the water, lower the heat, cover and cook for about 1 1/2 hours, until tender. Add the potatoes and tomatoes and cook for 20 minutes more. Preheat the broiler. Meanwhile, beat the egg with the milk and fold in the breadcrumbs. Season with salt, pepper, and poultry seasoning, and moisten with a little of the pot roast juices, if necessary. Pat the dressing mixture over the meat and set under the broiler for a few minutes, until the dressing turns golden-brown.

Virginia Beef Stew

Serves 6

Dumplings were always an economical way to bulk up a meat stew.

2 pounds beef shank, cut into 1-inch cubes	6 carrots, peeled and chopped
1/4 cup seasoned flour	salt and pepper
2 tablespoons oil or shortening	**For the dumplings:**
6 small onions, peeled	2 cups flour
6 potatoes, peeled and quartered	4 teaspoons baking powder
	1/2 teaspoon salt
	1 cup milk or water

Dredge the beef in the seasoned flour. Heat the oil in a casserole and brown the beef well. Season with salt and pepper, add enough cold water to cover, and bring to a simmer. Cover and simmer for 2 hours. Add the onions, potatoes, and carrots, and cook for 20–30 minutes more. Meanwhile, combine the dumpling ingredients in a bowl. Fifteen minutes before serving, drop the mixture by spoonfuls into the stew. Cover and cook for 15 minutes. Serve at once.

Chili Short Ribs

Serves 4–6

Short ribs, or spare ribs, were not commonly eaten before the war. However, being an economical cut of meat, wartime cookery writers promoted their use with tasty recipes that were "as good nutritionally as they were delicious."

3 pounds spareribs	1 teaspoon chili powder
1/3 cup flour	1/4 teaspoon garlic salt
1/4 cup sliced onions	3 tablespoons brown sugar
2 cups canned tomatoes,	1 tablespoon horseradish
drained with juices	1 medium-sized cabbage,
reserved	cored and cut into
2/3 cup vinegar	eighths
2 teaspoons Worcestershire	salt and pepper
sauce	

Preheat the oven to 350°F and grease a casserole dish. Sprinkle both sides of the spareribs with salt and pepper, then dredge with flour. Place half of the ribs in the bottom of the casserole. Cover with onions and top with the remaining spareribs. In a bowl, combine the reserved tomato juice, vinegar, Worcestershire sauce, chili powder, garlic salt, brown sugar and horseradish, and pour over the ribs. Cover and bake for 2 hours, basting frequently. Remove the cover and push the cabbage between the layers of ribs. Sprinkle liberally with salt and pepper, baste with the cooking juices, and cook for 30 minutes more (uncovered). Add the canned tomatoes and cook for 30 minutes more, basting occasionally, until the meat separates easily from the bone and the cabbage is tender.

Banana Meat Loaf

Serves 4

This unusual recipe is from the Antigonish Casket.

4 bananas, peeled	1/2 teaspoon dry mustard
1 pound ground beef	2 strips of bacon
1 cup soft breadcrumbs	salt and pepper
1 tablespoon finely chopped	
onion	

Preheat the oven to 350°F and grease a baking pan. Mash two of the bananas in a bowl, and mix with the ground beef, breadcrumbs, onion, and mustard. Season with salt and pepper. Shape the mixture into a loaf, and place on the prepared baking pan. Lay the strips of bacon on top. Bake for 40 minutes. Slice the remaining two bananas lengthwise and lay them on top of the loaf. Baste with the pan juices and cook for 20 minutes more. Remove from the oven and allow to cool for 5 minutes before slicing.

Hamburger Muffins

Serves 8

1 pound ground beef	1/2 teaspoon poultry
1 1/2 cups dry breadcrumbs	seasoning
1/2 cup milk	water
3 tablespoons oil	salt and pepper
2 tablespoons finely chopped	
onion	

Preheat the oven to 300°F and grease an 8-cup muffin pan. Combine the ground beef, 1/2 cup breadcrumbs, and milk. Season with salt and pepper and set aside. Heat the oil in a frying pan and sauté the onion. Stir in the remaining breadcrumbs, poultry seasoning, and enough water to moisten. Shape the ground meat mixture into 16 thin patties. Sandwich 2 patties together with a spoonful of stuffing, pressing the edges to seal. Place each stuffed patty into a greased muffin cup. Bake for 35 minutes.

14

Dinner in a Dish

Serves 6–8

4 tablespoons oil or shortening	1 egg, beaten
1 onion, chopped	2 cups canned corn
1 green pepper, seeded and chopped	1 2/3 cups canned tomatoes
1 pound ground beef	1/3 cup buttered bread-crumbs
	salt and pepper

Preheat the oven to 350°F and grease a shallow baking dish. Heat the oil or shortening and sauté the onion and green pepper. Stir in the ground beef and brown well. Remove from heat and beat in the egg and seasonings. Place a third of the mixture in the bottom of the prepared dish. Add half of the corn and then half of the tomatoes. Repeat the layers, ending with a layer of meat. Scatter the breadcrumbs over top and bake for 35 minutes.

Creamed Turkey

Serves 4

2 cups cold diced turkey	1/4 cup peas
1 tablespoon butter	1/4 cup diced celery
2 tablespoons flour	1 tablespoon chopped pimento
1 can mushroom soup	

Melt butter, add the flour, and blend well. Add the can of soup and simmer until the flour is cooked. Now add the peas, celery, pimento, and turkey and heat over boiling water in a double boiler. If desired, add a little salt and pepper to taste. Serve this creamed dish in a mold of steamed rice or macaroni. To make a sauce to serve with this dish, put equal amounts of cranberries, orange rind, and pulp through the chopper and sweeten slightly with honey.

Beef Upside Down Pie

Serves 8

This recipe appeared in a 1940s Magic Baking Powder newspaper advertisement, and promised to be "quick, thrifty, and delicious"—everything a wartime housewife wanted.

1 1/2 cups flour	1/4 cup sliced onions
3 teaspoons baking powder	1/2 pound ground beef
1 teaspoon celery salt	1 can of condensed tomato
1/2 teaspoon white pepper	soup
5 tablespoons shortening	
3/4 cup milk	

Preheat the oven to 475°F and grease a pie plate. Sift together the flour, baking powder, celery salt, and pepper in a mixing bowl. Cut in 3 tablespoons of shortening, and stir in the milk. Melt the remaining shortening in a frying pan, and sauté the onions until softened. Add the ground beef and brown well. Stir in the tomato soup, and spoon the mixture into the prepared dish. Press the pastry mixture on top and bake for 20–25 minutes, until browned. Invert the dish onto a serving platter and turn out the "pie." Serve hot.

Sausage Chowder

Serves 6

2 1/2 cups diced potatoes	2 1/2 tablespoons flour
1/2 cup diced celery	3 1/2 cups milk
1 onion, finely chopped	salt and pepper
1/2 pound sausages, chopped in small pieces	

Combine the potatoes, celery, and onion in a saucepan with a little salted water. Bring to a boil and cook for 15 minutes, until tender. Meanwhile, fry the chopped sausages in a large skillet until cooked through. Pour off all but 3–4 tablespoons of the fat. Stir in the flour and cook for 1 minute. Add the milk and bring to a simmer, stirring constantly until thickened. Add the cooked vegetables along with the pot liquid. Season with salt and pepper and serve hot.

Emergency Special

Serves 8

It was not unusual in Halifax to have unexpected guests for dinner. The city was teeming with military personnel, in training or on leave, and people liked to offer "their boys" a home-cooked meal. Fortunately, ground beef could stretch a long way when necessary.

1 1/2 pounds ground beef	2 tablespoons flour
1 small onion, finely chopped	1 cup milk
1/2 cup fine dry breadcrumbs	1/2 teaspoon salt
1 egg, beaten	dash pepper
3 tablespoons oil	

Combine the ground beef, onion, breadcrumbs, and beaten egg. Season with salt and form into small patties. Heat the oil in a skillet and fry for 2–3 minutes per side, to brown. Remove from the pan and set aside. Add the flour and cook for 1 minute, scraping any browned bits from the bottom of the pan. Stir in the milk and bring to simmer. Cook for 5 minutes, stirring constantly, until thickened. Return the patties to the pan and simmer for 5–10 minutes more, until cooked through. Serve hot.

Sausage and Sweet Potato Cobbler

Serves 4–6

8 pork sausages	3/4 cup flour
2 cups unsweetened	1 3/4 teaspoons baking
applesauce, drained	powder
2 cups diced cooked sweet	1/2 teaspoon salt
potatoes	1/2 cup milk

Preheat the oven to 450°F. Fry 6 sausages, remove from the pan, and slice. Use pan drippings to grease a casserole dish. Combine the applesauce, sweet potatoes, and cooked sausage slices and spoon into the prepared dish. In a separate bowl, sift together the flour, baking powder, and salt. Stir in the remaining pan drippings along with the milk. Press the mixture on top of the sweet potato and sausage mixture. Slice the remaining 2 sausages and arrange over top. Bake for 30–40 minutes. Serve hot.

Sausage U-Boats

Serves 4

4 large baking potatoes	2 cups water
1 pound sausages	2 tablespoons flour

Preheat the oven to 450°F and bake the potatoes for 45 minutes, or until tender. Remove from the oven and leave until cool enough to handle. Meanwhile, prick the sausages with a fork. Place them in a warm skillet and add 1 cup water. Cover and simmer for 5 minutes. Drain, then increase the heat and fry the sausages until browned and cooked through. Reserve 1 tablespoon of the drippings. Slice four sausages in half lengthwise, and roughly chop the rest. Halve the cooled potatoes lengthwise, and scoop the flesh from the skins. Mash the flesh with the chopped sausages, then divide the mixture between the 8 "boats." Top each boat with a sliced half-sausage. Return to the oven for 10 minutes to heat through. Meanwhile, blend the flour into the reserved sausage drippings in the frying pan, and cook for 1 minute. Gradually add 1 cup water, bring to a boil, and simmer until thickened. Pour the gravy over the potato boats and serve at once.

Sunshine Liver

Serves 6

1 pound beef or pork livers	4 tablespoons seasoned flour
3 cups stale breadcrumbs	melted fat or oil
1/2 cup minced onion	salt and pepper
1 egg, beaten	

Preheat the oven to 400°F and grease a 6-cup muffin pan. Bring a pot of lightly salted water to the boil and add the livers. Remove from heat and let stand 5 minutes. Drain and put through a meat grinder (or chop finely in a food processor). Mix the liver with the breadcrumbs, onion, and egg. Season with salt and pepper, and shape into 6 patties. Roll patties in the seasoned flour, and push them into the prepared muffin cups. Brush with melted fat or oil and bake 10 minutes.

Baked Liver Creole

Serves 4–6

1 pound sliced beef livers	1 can of crushed tomatoes
1/4 pound sliced bacon	1/4 cup chili sauce or green
1 large onion, sliced	relish
2 tablespoons seasoned flour	Worcestershire sauce

Preheat the oven to 350°F and grease a shallow baking dish. Bring a pot of lightly salted water to the boil and add the livers. Remove from heat and let stand 5 minutes before draining. Arrange a layer of bacon in the prepared baking dish. Add a layer of liver, followed by a layer of onions. Sprinkle with the seasoned flour. Repeat the layers, ending with a layer of bacon. In a bowl, combine the tomatoes with the chili sauce or relish and a dash of Worcestershire sauce. Pour over the liver, cover, and bake for 35 minutes. Remove the cover and bake 10 minutes more, until browned.

Savoury Liver Rolls

Serve 4–6

1–1 1/2 pounds calf liver, cut into eight 1/4-inch-thick slices	2 tablespoons oil
	1 tablespoon flour
	1/2 cup white wine or water
8 fresh sage leaves	salt and pepper
8 slices of bacon	

Season the liver with salt and pepper. Roll up the slices and wrap a sage leaf then a slice of bacon around each, securing with toothpicks. Heat the oil in a frying pan and fry the rolls until the liver is tender and the bacon is crisp. Remove from the pan and keep warm. Stir the flour into the pan, scraping up any browned bits. Cook for 1 minute, and add the wine or water. Bring to a boil and cook until thickened. Pour over the liver rolls and serve at once.

Pork and Parsnip Stew

Serves 4

1 tablespoon oil or shortening	3 cups boiling water
1 pound trimmed pork loin or shoulder, cut into 1-inch cubes	3 cups diced parsnips
	1 1/2 tablespoons flour
	3 tablespoons minced parsley
	salt
1 onion, minced	

Heat the oil in a skillet and brown the pork. Stir in the onion and cook for 3 minutes. Add the water, cover, and simmer gently for about 1 hour, until tender. Stir in the parsnips and cook 10–15 minutes more. Make a paste with the flour and a little of the cooking liquid, and stir into the pan. Season with salt, and cook, stirring constantly, until the stew has thickened. Sprinkle with parsley and serve.

Chicken Pot Pie with Dumplings

Serves 6

4 pounds stewing chicken	**For dumplings:**
3 quarts boiling water	1 cup flour
2 tablespoons salt	1 teaspoon baking powder
1 tablespoon sage or poultry seasoning	1/2 teaspoon salt
2 carrots	2 tablespoons butter
1/2 pound small onions	1/2 cup milk

Wash chicken. Cut into joints. Place in a large pot. Add boiling water, salt, and sage. Bring to a boil, cover, lower heat, and simmer for 2-3 hours until tender. Add carrots, sliced thick, and onions. Continue cooking while mixing dumplings. **For dumplings:** Sift together flour, baking powder, and salt. Cut the butter into the flour, and stir in just enough milk to make a soft but not sticky dough. Roll out to 1/4 thickness; cut in little round circles (use a small biscuit cutter for this). Drop the cut dumplings into the quickly boiling stew. Cover tightly, turn heat low so that the pot will not boil over, then boil for 10 minutes without lifting the lid. To serve, lift chicken, dumplings and vegetables onto a large platter. If gravy is not sufficiently thickened, mix 2 tablespoons of flour with water to make a smooth paste. Stir into broth. Cook until smooth and creamy.

Glazed Baked Ham

Serves 10–12

In the 1940s, as now, hams came both fully or partially cooked. Fully cooked hams need only be heated through, which takes about 10–12 minutes per pound. Partially cooked hams take a little longer to cook through (15–20 minutes per pound). While they aren't as popular today, fifty years ago "country hams" were very common. They were dry-cured and salted, and needed to be soaked in cold water for 24 hours and simmered slowly (25–30 minutes per pound) before being baked and glazed. Either glaze will work with any of the above: cook your ham according to package directions.

5–15-pound ham (bone-in)
whole cloves
For Orange Glaze:
1 cup orange juice
1 tablespoon grated orange
    zest
1 cup brown sugar
orange slices, to garnish

For Honey-Pineapple Glaze:
3/4 cup pineapple juice
3/4 cup liquid honey
1/2 teaspoon dry mustard
maraschino cherries, to
    garnish

Bake the ham according to package directions. Heat the glaze ingredients in a small saucepan until melted and thickened. Regardless of the kind of ham you are using, 45 minutes before it is ready, remove the rind and pour off most of the fat from the pan. Score the surface in a grid pattern, using a sharp knife. Push the whole cloves into the scored surface. Brush the ham with the glaze, then return it to the oven and continue baking. Baste frequently with the glaze, and allow the ham to rest for 20 minutes before carving. Garnish each plate according to the glaze used.

Roosevelt Chicken

Serves 6

Another meat and banana combination, this recipe was named in honour of the American president after the Yankees joined the war. It must have been a real celebration dish, given the sherry and the unusual quantity of butter required.

1/2 cup butter
6 chicken breasts, skins removed
3 whole bananas, peeled and halved lengthwise
1 tablespoon flour

1/2 cup cooking sherry or white grape juice
2 cups cream
salt and pepper
6 pieces of toast, to serve

Preheat the oven to 350°F and butter a shallow baking dish. Arrange the sliced bananas in the dish. Heat 2 tablespoons of butter in a frying pan and sauté the chicken breasts until brown. Place each chicken breast on top of a banana slice and bake for 40–45 minutes, until cooked through.

Meanwhile, melt the remaining butter in the frying pan and add the flour. Cook for 1 minute, scraping up any browned bits from the bottom of the pan. Add the sherry or grape juice, and bring to a boil. Reduce the heat and stir in the cream. Cook gently, stirring constantly, until the sauce has thickened. Season with salt and pepper.

Place the toasts on individual serving plates, set a chicken breast (along with the banana) on each, and pour the cream sauce over top.

Hot Chicken Loaf with Mushroom Sauce

Serves 4 to 6

3 pounds chicken	1 teaspoon salt
4 eggs	2 tablespoons pimento, cut in
melted butter or margarine	strips
1 cup fine breadcrumbs	1/4 teaspoon paprika
1 celery stalk with few leaves	1/8 teaspoon pepper
2 small carrots	dash of celery salt
1 thin slice of onion	2 tablespoons minced onion

Cook chicken in a small amount of water with celery, carrots, and onion. Cut meat from bones in long shreds; measure (there should be 4 cups or more) into a bowl. Add remaining ingredients except eggs, butter or margarine, and crumbs. Beat eggs until light and foamy and stir into chicken mixture. Gently form into a loaf; do not press. Place in a well-greased baking dish. Brush with melted butter or margarine. Press crumbs on loaf. Set in a pan of hot water. Bake at 400°F for 30 minutes.

For Sauce:

1/4 pound of mushrooms or	1/4 cup flour
1 small can	1/2 cup mushroom liquid
1/4 cup melted butter or	1/2 teaspoon salt
margarine	dash of pepper

Wash and peel mushrooms. Remove stems. Place mushrooms in a saucepan, add water and simmer for 10 minutes or until tender. Drain, reserving liquid. Blend butter or margarine with flour in saucepan. Add stock liquid and salt and pepper. Cook 10 minutes or until thickened. Add mushrooms and heat. Serve over chicken loaf.

Roast Lamb with Currant Sauce

Serves 8

Although lamb was not available very often—and was twice the price of beef—grocery stores occasionally advertised specials, such as Dominion's 1944 newspaper ad for "Genuine 1944 Spring" legs of lamb. This recipe didn't use wine for the basting sauce, but substituted the more economical grape juice.

1 lamb shoulder (4–5 pounds boneless, or 8–9 pounds bone-in)	8 strips of bacon
	1/2 cup currant jelly
	salt and pepper
1 tablespoon butter	1 small can of sliced
1/4 cup seasoned flour	pineapple, to serve
1 cup grape juice	

Preheat the oven to 350°F. Rub the butter over the lamb and dredge in the seasoned flour. Roast for 2–2 1/4 hours (up to 3 1/2 hours if bone-in), basting every 15 minutes with the grape juice. Thirty minutes before the lamb is cooked, roll up the bacon strips, securing them with toothpicks, and place alongside the lamb. When done, remove the lamb from the oven, transfer to a hot serving platter, and let stand 10 minutes before carving. Meanwhile, drain the pan juices into a saucepan and enrich with the currant jelly and extra grape juice, if necessary. Bring to a simmer and season to taste. Garnish the lamb with the bacon curls and sliced pineapple, and serve with the currant sauce.

No More Lobster, Please!

Fish and Seafood

No More Lobster, Please!

The war had far-reaching consequences for the Maritime fishing industry. Some 500 fishing vessels were commandeered by the government, and many fishermen left their jobs to join the services. Canned salmon and tuna virtually disappeared from the shelves of most grocery stores during the war years, as these were needed for the "boys overseas." Housekeepers were urged instead to purchase mackerel or flounders, which prior to the war were considered undesirable. When fresh salmon was available, local grocery stores such as Sobey's and Dominion gave it a prominent place in their newspaper and in-store advertisements.

On the other hand, fresh lobster was frequently seen on local wartime menus. It was both cheap and widely available. In fact, it is not uncommon to hear elderly Maritimers complain that they ate so much lobster during the war years that they can't bear even to look at it today!

Mid-century housewives were particularly fastidious about cooking smells, and food writers offered many tips on how to deal with the unpleasant odours of raw fish. Two frequently-made suggestions were to rub one's hands with salt after handling fish, then to wash them in soapy water, or to add a generous quantity of raw mustard seed to the dishwater to remove fish odour from dishes and pans.

Baked Fish with Lemon Celery Dressing

Serves 6

6 cups stale bread cubes	1 cup hot water
1 cup chopped celery	2 tablespoons lemon juice
1/2 cup chopped green	1/4 cup melted butter
pepper	1 1/2–2 pounds fresh halibut
1/2 cup chopped stuffed	or salmon steaks
olives	salt and paprika

Preheat the oven to 350°F and grease a shallow baking dish. Combine the bread cubes, celery, green pepper, olives, hot water, lemon juice, and all but 1 tablespoon of the melted butter. Place the mixture in the prepared dish and arrange the fish on top. Brush with the reserved butter and season with salt and paprika. Bake for 30 minutes.

Canadian Haddock en Crème

Serves 6

"Kipper snacks" are fillets of smoked herring, which you can buy at most grocery stores.

1 1/2 pounds haddock fillets	1 tablespoon grated onion
1/4 cup seasoned flour	1 1/2 tablespoons minced
3 tablespoons butter	parsley
6 kipper snacks, chopped	3/4 cup cream

Preheat the oven to 375°F and grease a shallow casserole. Dredge the fish fillets in seasoned flour, and roll them up, securing each with a toothpick. Melt the butter and sauté the kipper snacks for 2–3 minutes. Add the rolled fillets, and brown lightly. Arrange in the prepared baking dish and sprinkle with the onion, parsley, and cream. Cover and bake for 25–30 minutes.

Fish Salad in Cranberry Rings

Serves 6–8

2 cups cranberries
1 cup boiling water
4 teaspoons gelatin, softened
   in 1/4 cup cold water
1/3 cup sugar
a pinch of salt
3/4 cup finely chopped celery

3/4 cup diced apple
1 1/2 cups flaked fish
1/3 cup Club French dressing
   (see page 45)
lettuce leaves or watercress,
   to serve

Cook the cranberries in the boiling water until the skins pop, then force them through a strainer into a mixing bowl. Add the softened gelatin with the sugar and a pinch of salt, stirring until dissolved. Pour into 6 or 8 individual ring moulds, and chill until firm. Meanwhile, toss the celery, apple, and flaked fish with the French dressing. Turn out each cranberry mould onto a bed of lettuce or watercress. Fill the centres with the fish salad.

Fish Loaf

Serves 6–8

The wartime imperative of not wasting food meant that cooks had to be creative in using leftovers. In this case, breakfast cereal is put to good use to stretch a small quantity of cooked fish. Serve this loaf with a mustard-flavoured white sauce.

3 cups corn flakes, crushed
   finely
1 1/2 cups milk
2 cups cooked white fish,
   flaked and chopped
1/3 cup sour cream
1 tablespoon lemon juice

1 tablespoon fresh chives or
   minced onion
1/4 teaspoon dried thyme
1 tablespoon chopped parsley
1 tablespoon salt
a dash of pepper
2 eggs, beaten

Preheat the oven to 375°F and grease a large loaf pan. Combine the corn flakes and milk in a bowl and let stand for 10 minutes. Beat in the remaining ingredients, except for the eggs. Fold in the beaten eggs, and then turn the mixture into the prepared pan. Bake for 1 hour.

Fish Cakes

This recipe was submitted to The Halifax Mail *by Mrs. Donald K. Munroe of West River Station, NB.*

2 potatoes, peeled and chopped	1 egg, beaten
3/4 cup chopped fresh cod filets	salt and pepper
	fat, for deep-frying

Place the potatoes in a pan and cover with cold water. Bring to a boil and cook for 15 minutes. Add the fish and cook for 5 minutes more. Drain well, and mash the potatoes and fish with the beaten egg and seasoning. Shape into patties and deep-fry until golden-brown. Serve hot.

Shrimp Luncheon Rolls

Serves 4

1 1/4 cups shrimp
1/2 cup chopped celery
1 cup cooked (or canned) chopped green beans or peas
1 cup Club French dressing (see page 53)
salt and pepper

To serve:
4 large soft rolls
mayonnaise (see page 36)
salad greens (optional)

Combine the shrimp, celery, and beans or peas. Toss in the dressing, season with salt and pepper, and chill for 30 minutes. Drain well. Split the rolls and spread with mayonnaise. Divide the shrimp mixture between the rolls, adding salad greens if desired.

Shrimp Creole

Serves 4

It was fashionable during the war to serve moulded dishes, and rice was often formed into a ring rather than simply dished out from the pot. This shrimp dish would commonly be served in the centre of such a rice ring.

4 tablespoons butter
1 onion, sliced
1 pound mushrooms, sliced
2 pounds cooked shrimp
1 can of tomatoes
1 small bottle of pimento-
    stuffed olives, drained
    and chopped
salt and pepper

Melt the butter in a frying pan and sauté the onions for 5 minutes. Add the mushrooms and cook over low heat, stirring constantly, until tender and lightly browned. Add the shrimp, tomatoes, salt, and pepper, and simmer for 10 minutes. Stir in the olives and cook 5 minutes more. Serve hot.

Scalloped Oysters

Serves 4–6

This recipe stretches a dozen oysters by supplementing them with eggs and noodles.

1/4 pound egg noodles
3 tablespoons butter
3 tablespoons flour
1 1/2 cups milk
2 tablespoons chopped
    parsley
1/4 teaspoon mace
salt and cayenne pepper
4 hardboiled eggs, sliced
1 dozen oysters
buttered breadcrumbs

Preheat the oven to 400°F and grease a baking dish. Cook the noodles in lightly salted boiling water for 6–8 minutes. Drain.

Meanwhile, melt the butter in a saucepan and stir in the flour. Cook for 1 minute. Gradually add the milk, and bring to a simmer. Cook for 5–10 minutes, stirring constantly, until thickened. Stir in the parsley and seasonings, and remove from heat. Arrange half the noodles, sliced eggs, and oysters in the prepared dish. Pour half the sauce over top, then repeat the layers, ending with the sauce. Sprinkle with buttered breadcrumbs and bake for 15 minutes, until browned.

Oysters Indienne

1 box of frozen oysters, thawed	1 1/2 tablespoons flour
4 tablespoons butter	1 teaspoon curry powder
cream	salt and pepper

Melt half the butter in a skillet and sauté the oysters until the edges begin to curl. Remove from heat and drain, reserving the cooking liquid and setting the oysters aside. Add enough cream to the reserved liquid to make up one cup. Melt the remaining butter in the skillet and stir in flour and seasonings. Cook for 1 minute, stirring constantly. Add the cream and cook over low heat until thickened, stirring frequently. Stir in the oysters and cook until heated through.

Lobster Croquettes

Recipes for croquettes appeared frequently in wartime newspaper and magazine food columns. They were encouraged as a tasty and economical way to make a little go a long way. While mashed potatoes were a popular base for croquettes, the surplus of lobster in the Maritimes meant that recipes like this one were in great demand.

White Sauce:	1/2 teaspoon salt
2 tablespoons butter	pinch of pepper
2 tablespoons flour	1 cup milk

In saucepan melt butter. Blend in flour, salt and pepper. Gradually stir in milk. Cook, stirring constantly, until thick.

Croquettes:	1 tablespoon finely chopped
12 ounces cooked lobster	watercress
1 cup cold white sauce	salt and cayenne pepper
1 egg yolk, beaten	1 cup fine cracker crumbs
1 teaspoon lemon juice	oil, for deep-frying

Remove the claws from the lobster meat and set aside. Chop the remaining flesh and mix well with the white sauce, egg yolk, lemon juice, watercress, and seasonings. Shape the mixture into cutlets, roll in the cracker crumbs, and deep-fry until golden-brown. Insert a lobster claw into each croquette before serving. Serves 6.

Creamed Lobster in Potato Ring

Serves 8–10

Although extravagant dinner parties were viewed as frivolous and unbecoming to wartime behaviour, the war brought with it the need to entertain visiting personnel and soldiers on leave. People would club together to share their rations for special occasions, or simply use their imaginations to make a little go a long way.

1/2 cup crushed corn flakes	**For the creamed lobster:**
12 potatoes, peeled and	2 tablespoons butter
chopped	2 tablespoons flour
3/4 cup milk	1 cup milk
salt and pepper	1 cup cooked lobster meat,
1 cup cooked peas, to serve	chopped
	salt and pepper

Preheat the oven to 350°F and grease a 9-inch ring-mould. Line the mould with the crushed corn flakes and set aside. Cook the potatoes in lightly salted boiling water, then drain and mash them with the milk, until light and fluffy. Season to taste with salt and pepper. Pack the mashed potatoes into the prepared ring-mould and bake for 20 minutes.

Meanwhile, melt the butter in a saucepan and stir in the flour. Cook for 1 minute. Gradually add the milk, bring to a simmer, and cook for 5–10 minutes, stirring constantly until thickened. Stir in the chopped lobster and season with salt and pepper.

Invert the ring-mould onto a serving platter and carefully turn out the potato ring. Spoon the cooked peas around the outside edge and fill the centre with the creamed lobster. Serve hot.

New England Fish Chowder

Serves 6–8

1 pound whole cleaned fish or thick fillets	2 onions, minced
1/4 cup seasoned flour	3 potatoes, peeled and diced
1/2 cup diced salt pork	2 cups scalded milk
3 tablespoons fat	salt and pepper
	pilot biscuits, to serve

In a saucepan, cover the fish with cold water and bring to a simmer. Cook for 20 minutes. Strain the fish, reserving the cooking liquid and returning it the pan with enough boiling water to make up 4 cups of stock. Bring to a simmer. Meanwhile, cube the fish and dredge it in seasoned flour. In a frying pan, fry the salt pork in the fat until browned. Remove from the pan and add the onions. Sauté until golden-brown. Transfer the pork, onions, fish, and potatoes to the simmering stock. Cover and simmer, without stirring, until the potatoes and fish are tender. Add the scalded milk, and season to taste. Heat through and serve at once with crackers or tea biscuits (pilot biscuits would have been used during wartime).

New England Style Clam Chowder

Serves 6

4 cups shelled clams	2 cups cold water
1 cup 1/2-inch cubes of salt pork	2 1/2 cups scalded milk
3/4 cup sliced onion	1/2 cup light cream or evaporated milk
4 cups sliced potatoes	2 tablespoons butter

Drain and chop the clams, reserving both juices and clams. Meanwhile, in a large pot, fry the pork until almost crisp. Add the sliced onions, and cook for 5 minutes, until softened but not browned. Stir in the potatoes, and add the water and clam juice. Bring to a simmer and cook for 10 minutes. Add the chopped clams and simmer gently for about 15 minutes, or until the potatoes are tender. Gradually add the scalded milk and cream or evaporated milk. Heat through, then stir in the butter. Serve immediately.

Sauces for Hot Fish

Makes 1 cup

Whether boiled, broiled, or baked, fish was almost always served with a sauce. The following "drawn butter" sauce had a number of variations, given below.

3 1/2 tablespoons butter	1 teaspoon lemon juice
2 tablespoons flour	salt and pepper
1 cup hot water or fish stock	

In a small saucepan, melt 2 tablespoons of butter. Stir in the flour and cook for 1 minute. Gradually add the water or stock, stirring until thickened. Add the lemon juice and remaining butter, and season with salt and pepper.

Mustard Sauce: Omit the final 1 1/2 tablespoons of butter, and stir in 1/2 teaspoon prepared mustard.

Sauternes Sauce: Stir in 2 tablespoons Sauternes or other white wine before serving.

Egg Sauce: Fold in 1 sliced or chopped hardboiled egg before serving.

Shrimp or Lobster Sauce: Fold in 1/2 cup of chopped, cooked shrimp or lobster meat before serving.

Onion Sauce: Sauté a finely chopped onion in the fat before adding the flour.

Mock Hollandaise: Substitute milk for water or stock, and beat in 2 egg yolks before serving.

Cheese Sauce: Stir in 1/2 cup grated cheese before serving, and season to taste with Madeira or other wine.

Sauces for Cold Fish

Cold fish was often served at lunch with one of the following cold sauces.

Cucumber Sauce

Makes 3/4 cup

1 cup chopped cucumber,
  drained
1/2 teaspoon grated onion

1 tablespoon vinegar
salt and pepper

Mix ingredients lightly and chill.

Savoury Sauce

Makes 1 3/4 cup

1 cup mayonnaise (see page
  44)
1/4 cup chopped parsley
1/3 cup chopped chives

1/2 cup chopped watercress
2 teaspoons grated onion
1 tablespoon herb or tarragon
  vinegar

Mix all the ingredients. Chill until serving.

Victory Mayonnaise

Makes 2 1/2 cups

Mayonnaise was a popular dressing for salads and meat as well as fish. This recipe suggests using the fat rendered from a roast chicken, which adds flavour and economizes on salad oil. The mayonnaise "keeps well in the icebox," and can be thinned with milk or water, as desired.

2 tablespoons prepared mustard	3 eggs, beaten
1/2 tablespoon flour	1 cup milk
1 tablespoon salt	1 cup vinegar
	2/3 cup hot chicken fat

Combine the dry ingredients in the top of a double boiler. Stir in the eggs, milk, and vinegar until smooth. Gradually beat in the chicken fat and cook until thickened, stirring constantly.

Victory Gardens

Vegetables

Victory Gardens

Although fresh vegetables were not rationed in the Maritimes, families were encouraged to plant victory gardens in order to produce enough vegetables for their own use. This wartime initiative was driven both by the need to free up commercially grown produce for military consumption, as well as to advance the health—and thus the productivity—of the civilian labour force. Vegetables and fruits were near the top of the list in Canada's "Eat Right to Fight" program. Staying healthy was promoted as a moral imperative during wartime.

As always, the emphasis was on thrift. The Dominion Department of Agriculture developed a vigorous campaign promoting wartime gardens, and local horticultural societies and gardening clubs sponsored victory garden programs. Civilians were encouraged to share gardening implements with neighbours and to plan their gardens carefully, because "a garden that is not a success is a waste of materials and manpower, and we cannot afford waste." In addition to growing their own produce, women on the home front were advised to can surplus tomatoes, peas, and beans, as well as to store potatoes and other root vegetables for winter use. The fewer vegetables and fruits a housewife had to buy at the supermarket, the greater was her contribution to the war effort.

Generally speaking, vegetable recipes from this period are not particularly inspiring, given current sensibilities about simple preparation and minimal cooking. However, wartime food writers offered their readers many tips on how to use their home-grown vegetables to the greatest advantage. Some of these seem rather obvious, such as adding a teaspoon of sugar to the water when cooking corn to bring out its sweetness. Others are a little more unusual—braised cauliflower leaves, for example, which one writer suggested combines the flavours of Brussels sprouts and young cabbage. Canada's Health and Welfare department reminded housewives that two medium-sized potatoes, when steamed or baked in their skins, contain as much vitamin C as one orange. The keen victory gardener could even make use of rose hips and dandelion greens, which were also promoted as a valuable source of vitamin C.

Glazed Turnips

Serves 4–6

Here's a wartime recipe that still has good reason to be popular today.

1 pound young turnips	1 tablespoon sugar
2 tablespoons butter	1/2 cup stock or gravy
1/2 tablespoon flour	

Preheat the oven to 325°F. Cook the turnips in boiling salted water for 10 minutes. Drain well and dice. Melt the butter in an ovenproof skillet and sauté the turnips for 2 minutes. Sprinkle with the flour and sugar. When nicely browned, add the stock or gravy and cover the pan. Bake for 15 minutes, shaking the pan occasionally, until the turnips have absorbed the stock.

Mashed Potato Casserole

Serves 4

2 cups mashed potatoes	4 slices of bacon, cooked and
1/2 cup grated cheese	crumbled
	salt and pepper

Preheat the oven to 350°F. Season the mashed potatoes with salt and pepper, and spoon into a shallow baking dish. Scatter the cheese over top, followed by the bacon bits. Cook for 20 minutes, until the potatoes are heated through and the top is crisp.

Baked Corn and Tomatoes

Serves 6

2 cups cooked corn	1 cup fresh breadcrumbs
2 cups chopped tomatoes	2 tablespoons butter
1 teaspoon sugar	salt and pepper

Preheat the oven to 350°F and butter a shallow baking dish. Season the corn and tomatoes with sugar, salt, and pepper. Pour into the prepared dish, sprinkle with breadcrumbs, and dot with butter. Bake for 30 minutes. Serve hot.

Creamed Carrots and Peas

Serves 4

4 carrots, peeled and diced	3 tablespoons flour
1 cup fresh peas	1 1/2 cups milk
2 teaspoons sugar	salt and pepper
3 tablespoons butter	

Bring a pot of water to the boil and add the carrots, peas, and sugar. Cook for 10–15 minutes. Drain and set aside. Melt the butter in the saucepan and stir in the flour. Cook for 1 minute, then gradually add the milk. Bring to a simmer, stirring until thickened. Season with salt and pepper, and stir in the drained vegetables. Reheat gently and serve hot.

Onion Chowder

Serves 6

2 tablespoons shortening	1 tablespoon salt
3 cups sliced onions	2 cups milk
4 cups boiling water	1 cup grated cheese
2 cups diced potatoes	2 tablespoons minced parsley

Melt the shortening in a large pot and sauté the onions for 5 minutes. Add the boiling water, potatoes, and salt. Simmer until the vegetables are tender. Add the milk and bring back to a simmer. Stir in the grated cheese and parsley and serve at once.

Mushrooms in a Spinach Ring

Serves 4–6

This is one of those recipes that makes anyone under the age of sixty shake her head in disbelief. Such a lot of effort involved when one could just stir-fry the vegetables and be done with it!

2 cups spinach	2 eggs, beaten well
4 tablespoons melted butter	1 pound mushrooms, sliced
3 cups hot white sauce (see page 31)	salt and pepper

Preheat the oven to 350°F and set a roasting pan with 2 inches of water in the oven. Grease a medium-sized ring-mould. Cook the spinach in just the water that remains clinging to the leaves after rinsing. Drain and chop. Toss the spinach in half the melted butter, and season with salt and pepper. Fold in 1 cup of the white sauce along with the beaten eggs. Place the spinach in the prepared ring-mould, set it in the hot water bath, and bake until firm. Meanwhile, sauté the mushrooms in the remaining butter. Invert the mould onto a large serving platter and carefully turn out the spinach ring. Spoon the mushrooms into the centre and pour the remaining white sauce over top. Serve at once.

Cream of Vegetable-Barley Soup

Serves 6

1/3 cup barley	4 cups milk
2 onions, diced	1 tablespoon butter
2 carrots, peeled and diced	salt and pepper
2 potatoes, peeled and diced	
2 leaves of green cabbage, shredded	

In a large pan, cover the barley with boiling water and cook for about 30 minutes, until almost tender. Add the vegetables and enough water to keep them from burning. Simmer until tender. Stir in the milk and butter and bring to a simmer. Season to taste with salt and pepper. Serve hot.

Canned String Beans with Onions

Serves 4

This was one wartime cook's way to perk up canned beans.

4 cups canned string beans
1 onion, grated
1 onion, studded with whole
    cloves

2 tablespoons butter
salt and pepper

Combine the ingredients in a skillet, adding a little liquid from the canned beans. Cover and simmer for 20 minutes. Discard the whole onion before serving.

Savoury Summer Squash

Serves 4–6

Summer squash is what we generally call zucchini. It seems that even victory gardeners produced a surplus! The original recipe called for boiling the chopped squash for 20 minutes, which is at least twice as long as we would think of cooking it today.

6 cups chopped summer
    squash (zucchini)
1 can of condensed beef
    consommé

1 tablespoon butter
pepper

In a skillet, cover the squash with the consommé and 1 cup of boiling water. Cover and cook for 5–8 minutes, then remove the squash using a slotted spoon and bring the liquid to a boil. Cook until reduced to a 1/2 cup. Stir in the butter and season with pepper. Return the squash to the skillet and heat through. Serve at once.

California Beets

Serves 6

This recipe was submitted to The Halifax Mail *by Mrs. E. MacLeod of Summerside, PEI, Canada's own sunshine province.*

6 bunches of small beets	2 tablespoons lemon juice
1 tablespoon butter	1 tablespoon sugar
3 whole cloves	salt and pepper

Cut the beets from their stems and wash well. Place the beets in a skillet and cover with cold water. Bring to a boil and cook until tender. Drain. Plunge the beets into cold water for 3 minutes, then rub off the skins. Melt the butter in the skillet, and add the cloves, lemon juice, sugar, salt, and pepper. Return the beets to the pan to heat through. Serve hot.

Cabbage Salad

Serves 4

2 cups cabbage, finely shredded	3/4 cup mayonnaise (see page 36)
1 can of chopped pineapple, drained	salt and pepper
1 cup desiccated coconut	lettuce leaves and radishes, to serve

Rinse the cabbage in cold water and drain well. Toss lightly with the pineapple and coconut. Fold in the mayonnaise and season with salt and pepper. Spoon the mixture in neat mounds on a bed of crisp lettuce leaves, and garnish with radish roses.

Jellied Potato Salad

Serves 8–10

At the middle of the last century it was not quite fashionable to serve salads tossed higgledy-piggledy as we are used to doing. Instead, the ingredients were often mixed with gelatin and served in quivering moulds.

2 1/2 cups diced cooked potatoes	1 cucumber, sliced thinly
2 teaspoons grated onion	1/2 cup sliced radishes
2 tablespoons salad oil	1/2 cup thinly sliced celery
6 tablespoons vinegar	salt and pepper
1 package lemon-flavoured gelatin	**To serve:**
1 1/4 cups hot water	lettuce leaves
5 tablespoons mayonnaise (see page 36)	sliced devilled eggs
	Club French dressing (see page 45)

In a large bowl, combine the potatoes, onion, salad oil, and 3 tablespoons of vinegar. Season with salt and pepper, and leave for 25 minutes to marinate, stirring occasionally. Meanwhile, in another bowl, dissolve the gelatin in the hot water. Add 3 tablespoons of vinegar and a dash of salt. Measure out 2/3 cup of the gelatin mixture and stir in 3 tablespoons of cold water. Pour into a ring-mould or loaf pan, and chill until slightly thickened. Arrange a few cucumber, celery, and radish slices in the gelatin base and chill until quite firm. Chill the remaining gelatin until slightly thickened, then place the bowl in a basin of iced water and whisk until as fluffy and thick as whipped cream. Fold in the mayonnaise until combined, and fold in the remaining cucumber and radish slices. Drain the potatoes and fold them in as well. Pour into the set gelatin mould and chill until firm. Turn out onto a serving platter, garnish with a border of lettuce leaves and devilled eggs, and drizzle French dressing over top.

Club French Dressing

Makes 1 cup

This was a popular salad dressing which was served in place of mayonnaise or "salad cream."

3 tablespoons finely chopped
    onion
1 tablespoon sugar
1 tablespoon Worcestershire
    sauce
3 tablespoons tomato
    ketchup

4 tablespoons distilled white
    or pure cider vinegar
1/2 cup salad oil
1/2 teaspoon salt

Beat together the ingredients until emulsified. Chill until needed.

Savoury Vegetable Sauce

Makes 1 cup

This bread sauce was served over any cooked vegetable—cabbage, broccoli, green beans, carrots, etc.

2 tablespoons minced onion	1 1/4 cups milk
2 tablespoons drippings	a pinch of dried thyme
1/2 cup fine fresh bread- crumbs	salt and pepper

Sauté the minced onion in hot fat for 5 minutes. Stir in the bread-crumbs and sauté until golden-brown. Add the milk and seasonings, and simmer for 10 minutes, stirring frequently. Remove from heat and serve.

Cress and Dandelion Salad

Serves 4

1 cup watercress, rinsed well	Club French dressing (see
1 cup dandelion greens, rinsed well	page 45), to serve
1 small onion, sliced thinly	

Arrange the watercress and dandelion greens in a salad bowl. Add the onion slices, and pour the dressing over all.

Eat Hash and Like It!

Leftovers and Other Potluck

Eat Hash and Like It!

A 1940s newspaper advertisement for War Savings Stamps depicts a housewife dishing up supper to her children. The youngsters smile with enthusiasm as the mother declares to the reader, "As long as Jack is at war, we'll eat hash and like it .... We are at war. It costs a lot to win. It would cost everything to lose!"

Leftovers were the order of the day on the home front. But as one magazine columnist noted, although leftovers had to be saved for reasons of both patriotism and thrift, "dabs of this and that may also be conserved simply in the interests of good cookery." She went on to extol the virtues of chopped meat, "delicious in a salad or moulded in gelatin."

Given the fact that wartime housewives were already committed to the idea of thrift in the kitchen, it may seem strange to us that leftovers were even an issue. After all, wouldn't women have cooked just enough for each meal and no more? But one must keep in mind the fact that cooking and food-buying patterns in the 1940s were decidedly different than today, when many of us buy pre-packaged portions of chicken or meat for use in a single meal. Wartime shoppers were more likely to buy a whole bird or roast, which was cooked slowly to avoid shrinkage, then served up in a variety of ways throughout the week.

Aside from the ubiquitous hash, pasta and beans gained acceptance, if not popularity, during the war years. It would take another twenty years before grains and pulses became fashionable staples in Canadian kitchens, but as "meat stretchers" they did find their way into wartime recipes for casseroles and other potluck dishes.

Monday Shepherd's Pie

Serves 6

This recipe makes use of Sunday's roast dinner—the leftover meat and fat drippings, plus any vegetables that didn't get eaten.

6 sweet potatoes, peeled and chopped	2 tablespoons flour
1/3 cup evaporated milk	2 cups hot water
2 tablespoons fat	1 1/2 cups cooked vegetables
2 cups chopped cooked beef	salt and pepper

Preheat the oven to 350°F and grease a shallow baking dish. Place the sweet potatoes in a saucepan and cover with cold water. Bring to a boil and cook for 15–20 minutes, until tender. Drain, reserving 1/3 cup of the cooking water. Mash the potatoes with the reserved cooking water and the evaporated milk, and set aside. Melt the fat in a frying pan and add the chopped beef. Sprinkle with the flour, and cook for 1 minute. Stir in the hot water and cook until the gravy thickens. Fold in the vegetables, season with salt and pepper, and spoon the mixture into the prepared baking dish. Drop the mashed sweet potatoes on top by the spoonful, and bake for 20 minutes, until browned and heated through.

Vegetable Hash

Serves 4

1 cup cooked lima beans	1 cup cooked diced carrots
2 onions, chopped finely	4 tablespoons fat
2 cups mashed potatoes	salt and pepper

Combine the beans, onions, mashed potatoes, and carrots. Heat the fat in a frying pan, and spoon in the mash, spreading it evenly. Cover and cook over a low heat until brown on the bottom. Fold as you would an omelet, and serve at once.

Six O'Clock Casserole

Serves 4

Alongside picnic hams and wax beans, canned spaghetti was often featured in Sobey's newspaper advertisements from the 1940s. At 15 cents a can, it was considerably less expensive than a tin of steak and mushrooms, which cost 35 cents. Canned spaghetti could make the tail end of a roast chicken yield one more meal, and when the clock strikes six and dinner's not yet on the table, a quick casserole is a very good idea.

1 large can of cooked spaghetti in tomato sauce	1 cup cooked peas
	buttered breadcrumbs
1 cup cooked turkey or chicken, chopped	

Preheat the oven to 375°F. Empty half the can of spaghetti into a shallow baking dish. Combine the chopped meat and cooked peas and spoon over the spaghetti. Spread the remaining spaghetti evenly over top and sprinkle with the breadcrumbs. Bake for 20 minutes, until golden-brown and bubbling.

Normandy Beef Hash

Serves 4

1 tablespoon fat	1/2 cup diced potatoes
3 onions, chopped	1/2 cup meat stock
2 cups boiled beef, diced	salt and pepper

Heat the fat in a frying pan and sauté the onions until golden-brown. Add the beef and potatoes, and fry for 5 minutes more. Pour in the stock and cook for 10 minutes, until the potatoes are cooked. Season and serve hot.

Veal Curry

Serves 4

Although we tend to think of wartime food as bland, it was during this period that the average Canadian housewife began to experiment with spices in order to liven up leftover meats and vegetables.

1 tablespoon oil	1/2 teaspoon ground ginger
3/4 pound cooked, diced veal	1/4 cup cold water
1 large onion, chopped finely	1/2 tablespoon Worcestershire
3 stalks of celery, diced	sauce
1 apple, peeled, cored, and	2 tablespoons molasses
diced	3/4 cup meat stock
1 1/2 tablespoons curry	salt and pepper
powder	

Heat the oil in a skillet and sauté the diced veal and onions until lightly browned. Stir in the celery and apple and cook for 5 minutes longer. In a small bowl, mix together the curry powder and ginger. Stir in the water, Worcestershire sauce, molasses, and stock. Blend well and add to the skillet. Bring to a simmer, season with salt and pepper, and cook for 10 minutes, until the sauce has reduced. Serve hot over cooked rice.

Beans and Bacon

Serves 2

Even a can of beans could make a tasty supper dish for two when seasoned with a little mustard and sugar.

1 large can of baked beans	1 tablespoon brown sugar
1 teaspoon dry mustard	6 strips of bacon

Preheat the oven to 375°F. Pour the beans into a small baking dish and stir in the mustard and sugar. Lay the bacon strips over top and bake for 20 minutes, until the bacon is crisp.

Creamed Chicken

Serves 6

While some Canadian cities, including Toronto, saw poultry shortages during the war—due mostly to transportation problems—Maritimers seemed to enjoy their usual stocks of chicken and turkey.

1 cup chicken broth	1 tablespoon lemon juice
1 cup milk or cream	1 teaspoon vinegar
2 egg yolks	1 tablespoon chopped parsley
2 cups cooked chicken	salt and pepper
8 small cooked white onions	toast, to serve

Combine the chicken broth with the milk or cream in a skillet. Bring to a simmer over a low heat, and beat in the egg yolks. Cook, stirring constantly, until thickened. Add the chopped chicken, onions, lemon juice, vinegar, and parsley. Season to taste with salt and pepper. Simmer for 10 minutes, then spoon onto hot toast to serve.

Macaroni and Beef Casserole

Serves 4–6

We are used to pouring a liberal amount of oil into the cooking water when boiling pasta, but wartime cooks simply rubbed a bit of fat around the inside edge of the pot to prevent the water from boiling over.

2 cups macaroni	1/2 onion, chopped
1 1/2 cups cooked beef,	1 cup grated cheese
chopped	buttered breadcrumbs
2 cups gravy	salt and pepper

Preheat the oven to 350°F and grease a shallow baking dish. Cook the macaroni for 9 minutes in a pot of lightly salted boiling water. Drain and mix in the chopped beef, gravy, onion, and grated cheese. Season with salt and pepper and pour into the prepared baking dish. Cover with buttered breadcrumbs and bake for 20 minutes, until golden-brown and bubbling.

Lima Beans and Bacon

Serves 4

3 slices of bacon, chopped	2 cups cooked lima beans
2 onions, sliced	1 cup milk
1 sweet green pepper, seeded	salt and pepper
and sliced finely	

Preheat the oven to 350°F and grease a shallow baking dish. Fry the bacon until crisp, and remove from the pan. Sauté the onions and green pepper in the bacon fat until tender. Place a third of the lima beans into the prepared dish, and add a layer of the onions and pepper. Repeat the layers twice more, and scatter the bacon over top. Pour the milk over top and bake for about 20 minutes. Serve hot.

Moulded Chicken and Vegetable Salad

Serves 6

Gelatin was the wartime cook's secret weapon. She could mix a little into almost anything to create a moulded salad.

1 can of condensed chicken
    and rice soup
3/4 cup cooked chicken
1 egg, separated
2 teaspoons gelatin, softened
    in 3 tablespoons water
1/4 cup whipping cream
1 tablespoon lemon juice

1/2 cup cooked diced carrots
1/2 cup cooked diced celery
1/2 cup cooked green peas

To garnish:
lettuce leaves and sliced
    tomatoes or whole spiced
    peaches

Strain the chicken soup, reserving the liquid, and put the rice and other solids through a grinder with the cooked chicken. Set aside. Heat the liquid in the top of a double boiler. Beat the egg yolk into the soup and cook for 3–4 minutes. Remove from heat and stir in the softened gelatin until dissolved. Fold in the ground chicken mixture, the beaten egg white, whipping cream, lemon juice, carrots, celery, and peas. Pour into a greased mould and chill until firm. Turn out onto a bed of lettuce leaves and garnish with tomato slices or whole spiced peaches.

Stuffed Cabbage

Serves 6

Bologna and frankfurters weren't just for lunchtime sandwiches.

1 cabbage, cored	2 cups diced bologna or
3 tablespoons fat	frankfurters
1 small onion, chopped	1/4 cup vinegar
2 cups diced cooked potatoes	1 tablespoon mustard
1 cup diced tomatoes	salt and pepper
1 cup diced cooked carrots	

Preheat the oven to 425°F and butter a baking dish. In a saucepan, cover the cabbage with lightly salted boiling water. Bring to a simmer and cook just until tender. Meanwhile, heat the fat in a frying pan and sauté the onion until browned. Stir in the diced potatoes, tomatoes, carrots, and bologna or frankfurters. Season with vinegar, mustard, salt, and pepper. Set aside. When the cabbage is tender, drain well and leave until cool enough to handle. Scoop out the flesh, leaving a 1 1/2-inch shell. Chop the flesh and add to the vegetable and bologna mixture. Stuff the cabbage with the filling, and place in the baking dish. Spoon any excess filling around the cabbage. Bake for 10–15 minutes and serve hot.

Southern Rice and Peanut Loaf

Serves 8

This unusual recipe stretches the imagination as well as the stomach! The original recipe suggested garnishing the loaf with sliced hardboiled eggs and serving it with a hot cheese sauce.

2 cups rice	2 cups salted peanuts
2 cups water	2 eggs, slightly beaten
1 teaspoon salt	1 egg white
4 cups scalded milk	crushed corn flakes
1/4 cup soft butter	

Preheat the oven to 350°F and grease a large loaf pan. Combine the rice, water and salt in a large saucepan, and bring to a boil. Cover and simmer for 10 minutes. Stir in the milk and bring back to a simmer. Cover and cook for 15–20 minutes more, until the rice has absorbed most of the liquid. Remove from heat and beat in the butter, peanuts, and eggs. Spread the mixture in a greased loaf pan. Brush with egg white and sprinkle with crushed corn flakes. Bake for 35–40 minutes.

Victory is Sweeter than Sugar

Wartime Baking and Desserts

Victory is Sweeter than Sugar

In 1942 weekly sugar rations were reduced from twelve ounces per person to half a pound. Today, two pounds of sugar a week for a family of four might seem like a substantial—even excessive—amount, given both our awareness of nutritional values and our contemporary obsession with weight control. However, in the 1940s sugar was perceived not as an indulgence, but as an indispensable flavouring ingredient and a meaningful source of food energy. The term "empty calories" had yet to be invented, and the full-figured woman was admired rather than scorned. Moreover, more households than not relied on home baking, particularly during the war years. Just think: if we were to stop purchasing store-bought cookies, salad dressings, jams, and even bread, our sugar jars would empty far more quickly than they do.

Sugar rations were reduced due to increasing dangers in shipping and transportation—Canada did not produce enough sugar to meet its own needs. However, wartime housewives still managed to put all manner of sweet treats on the table. More than one family relied on the trick of keeping separate bowls for each member's weekly sugar ration, which each would dip into for their morning coffee or breakfast cereal. At the end of the week mother would collect all the bowls and combine what sugar was left to make something special. Housewives might also save their sugar rations from week to week to make a favourite dish—despite official warnings against having more than two weeks' supply of sugar on hand at any time—or turn to a variety of sugar substitutes. Maple syrup, which was not subject to rationing, was commonly used in Atlantic Canada, as were molasses and honey. The wartime homemaker also used honey or corn syrup as well as condensed milk as a sweetener.

Pies and Puddings

Apples, blueberries, and cranberries have always been plentiful in the Maritime provinces. Wartime housewives made good use of this natural bounty, and took advantage of canning sugar rations to put up preserves so that their families could enjoy fruit pies and puddings all year round. Many households grew raspberries, strawberries, and rhubarb in their victory gardens, and these were also preserved for the winter months. But it is the chiffon and cream pies that ring nostalgic to anyone who grew up between the thirties and fifties. Fluffy chiffon pies, which are generally custard-based and stiffened with gelatin, first appeared in recipe books in the late 1920s, and were wildly popular during the war years. No doubt a large part of their appeal was that they appeared to be more substantial than they actually were. Chiffon cakes, which relied on large quantities of eggs, had to wait until after the war to reappear on the dessert table.

Victory Pastry

Makes three 9-inch pie shells or three dozen 2-inch tart shells

3/4 cup lard	3 cups flour or 3 1/3 cups
1/2 cup boiling water	pastry flour
1 1/2 teaspoons salt	

Cream the lard and gradually beat in the boiling water. Cool slightly before adding the salt and flour, mixing with a quick cutting motion; do not stir. Chill before rolling out.

Whole Wheat Pastry

Makes three 9-inch pie shells or three dozen 2-inch tart shells

1 1/2 cups whole-wheat flour	3/4 cup lard
1 1/2 teaspoons salt	1/2 cup cold water

Mix together the flour and salt. Cut in the lard until the mixture forms pea-sized crumbs. Gradually add enough water until the dough clings together in a ball. Chill before rolling out.

Vanilla Wafer Pie Crust

Makes one 9-inch pie shell

The sweetness of the vanilla wafers makes additional sugar unnecessary.

1 cup of vanilla wafer crumbs
5 tablespoons melted butter

Mix together the crumbs and butter and press firmly into the bottom and sides of a 9-inch pie plate. Chill until firm, or bake at 350°F for 10–15 minutes.

Chocolate Mint Pie

Serves 6

In this recipe the meringue is folded directly into the pie filling in order to cut back the amount of sugar needed.

2 squares (2 ounces) unsweetened chocolate, chopped finely
1/2 cup boiling water
1 tablespoon powdered gelatin, softened in 1/4 cup cold water

2 egg yolks
1/2 cup + 2 tablespoons sugar
1/2 teaspoon salt
2 drops oil of peppermint
3 egg whites
9-inch baked pie shell

Melt the chocolate in the 1/2 cup of boiling water, beating until smooth. Remove from heat and stir in the softened gelatin, until dissolved. Beat the egg yolks with the 1/2 cup of sugar, salt, and chocolate mixture. Stir in the peppermint oil and chill until partially set. Whip the egg whites until stiff but not dry, and gradually beat in the remaining 2 tablespoons of sugar. Fold egg whites and sugar into the chocolate mixture until combined, pour into the baked pie shell, and chill until set.

Magic Fruit Cream Pie

Serves 6

Condensed milk was another popular ingredient that allowed wartime bakers to cut back on white sugar.

1 1/3 cups sweetened condensed milk	1 cup whipping cream
1/4 cup lemon juice	2 tablespoons powdered sugar
1 cup mixed sliced soft fruits (e.g., raspberries, strawberries, peaches, or bananas)	9-inch baked pie shell or cookie-crumb crust

Beat together the condensed milk and lemon juice until the mixture thickens, and fold in the prepared fruit. Pour into baked pie shell. Whip the cream until firm, and sweeten to taste with the powdered sugar. Spoon onto the pie, and use a knife tip to create decorative swirls. Chill for 2 hours before serving.

Cranberry Chiffon Pie

Serves 6

The addition of cranberries gives this recipe a decidedly Maritime twist.

1 tablespoon powdered gelatin, softened in 1/2 cup water	1 cup sugar
2 cups cranberries	1 tablespoon lemon juice
1/4 cup cold water	1/4 teaspoon salt
3 eggs, separated	9-inch pie shell
	1 cup whipped cream, to serve

Cook the cranberries in 1/4 cup of water until their skins pop open. Push them through a sieve, discarding the seeds and skins, and beat with the egg yolks and half the sugar in the top of a double boiler. Bring to a simmer and cook slowly, stirring frequently, until thickened. Stir in the softened gelatin, lemon juice, and salt. In a separate bowl, beat the egg whites until stiff but not dry, and whisk in the remaining sugar. Fold into the cranberry custard. Transfer to the pie shell and chill until firm. Spread whipped cream over top just before serving.

Cranberry Maple Syrup Pie

Serves 6–8

This is a quintessentially Maritime wartime recipe, combining two ingredients that never saw a ration card.

pastry for double-crust 9-inch pie	2 cups cranberries
1 tablespoon flour	milk, to glaze
1 cup maple syrup	

Preheat the oven to 400°F. Roll out half the pastry and fit into a 9-inch pie plate. Sprinkle the flour on the bottom of the pie crust, and pour in the maple syrup. Add the cranberries. Roll out the remaining pastry to cover the pie. Crimp the edges together and brush with milk. Bake for about 40 minutes. Cool before serving.

Ada's Apple-Lemon Pie

Serves 6

This recipe came from Mrs. H.B. Hawkins of Truro, NS, who submitted it to The Halifax Mail *in April 1945.*

pastry for double-crust 9-inch pie	juice and grated zest of 1 lemon
1 cup sugar	1 tablespoon melted butter
2 tablespoons flour	1/4 cup hot water
1 egg, separated	2 apples, peeled, cored, and grated

Preheat the oven to 375°F. Roll out half the pastry and fit into a 9-inch pie plate. In a large bowl, beat together the sugar, flour, egg yolk, and lemon juice and zest. Beat in the melted butter and hot water. Fold in the grated apple and stiffly beaten egg white. Roll out the remaining pastry to cover the pie. Crimp the edges together and bake for about 30 minutes.

Washington Pie

Serves 6–8

This pie recipe, which came from Mildred Smith of Wolfville, NS, is actually a cake. Note the gelatin, a popular substitute for butter or fat, in the filling.

1/4 cup fat
1/2 cup sugar
1 egg, beaten
1/2 teaspoon vanilla
1 1/3 cups flour
2 1/2 teaspoons baking
  powder
1/4 teaspoon salt
1/2 cup milk

For the filling:
1 teaspoon powdered gelatin
2 tablespoons orange juice
2 cups milk
1 tablespoon sugar
1/8 teaspoon salt

Prepare the filling at least 4 hours before you want to serve the cake. Soak the gelatin in the orange juice. Heat 1/2 cup of the milk in a saucepan and stir in the softened gelatin, sugar, and salt. Stir until dissolved, then add the remaining milk. Refrigerate until thickened, about 4 hours, stirring occasionally. Beat until thick and smooth.

Meanwhile, preheat the oven to 375°F and grease and flour two 8-inch layer cake pans. Cream the fat and sugar in a mixing bowl. Beat in the egg and vanilla, until smooth. Sift together the dry ingredients and fold into the batter, alternating with the milk. Pour the batter into the prepared pans and bake for 25–30 minutes. Allow to cool before turning out and sandwiching together with the filling.

Maple Apples

Serves 6

While these days many families skip dessert, sixty years ago a meal wouldn't have been complete without "something to follow." This is the kind of quick and easy sweet that a busy wartime housewife would have whipped together and popped into the oven while dinner was cooking.

6 firm, tart apples, peeled and cored	1 cup maple syrup
6 teaspoons butter	

Preheat the oven to 350°F. Place the apples in a casserole dish. Push a teaspoon of butter into the centre of each apple. Pour the syrup over and around the apples, cover, and bake for 30–45 minutes, until tender. Serve warm or cold.

Apple Cheese Cobbler

Serves 6

6 apples, peeled, cored, and sliced thickly	2 tablespoons fat
1/4 cup brown sugar	3/4 cup grated cheese
1 tablespoon butter	1 egg, beaten with 6 tablespoons milk
1 1/2 cups flour	1/4 cup sugar
2 teaspoons baking powder	2 tablespoons boiling water
1/4 teaspoon salt	1/2 teaspoon almond extract

Preheat the oven to 400°F and grease a shallow baking dish. Arrange the sliced apples in the prepared baking dish. Sprinkle with the brown sugar and dot with butter. To make the dough, sift together the flour, baking powder, and salt in a bowl. Cut in the fat and grated cheese. Stir in the beaten egg and milk, and pat the dough over the apples. Bake for 15 minutes. Meanwhile, combine the sugar, boiling water, and almond extract, stirring until the sugar dissolves. Pour over the pastry and bake for 15 minutes longer.

Corn Flake Banana Pudding

Serves 4–6

1 package vanilla or butterscotch pudding	1 large or 2 small bananas, peeled and chopped
2 cups milk	1/4 cup finely crushed corn flakes

Pour 2 cups cold milk into a bowl. Add the instant pudding. Beat with a whisk or electric mixer on low speed until well-blended, about 2 minutes. Fold in the bananas and spoon into individual serving dishes. Chill. Before serving, sprinkle with crushed corn flakes.

Quick Maple Pudding

Serves 6

1 tablespoon butter	2 teaspoons baking powder
3 tablespoons sugar	1/3 teaspoon salt
1 egg	1/2 cup milk
1 cup flour	1 cup maple syrup

Preheat the oven to 350°F and grease a shallow baking dish. In a bowl, cream the butter and sugar thoroughly and beat in the egg. Sift together the flour, baking powder, and salt, and add to the creamed mixture, alternating with the milk. Pour the maple syrup into the prepared baking dish and spoon the batter over top. Bake for 25–30 minutes. Serve hot.

Vanilla Ice Cream

Serves 6

2/3 cup condensed milk	1 1/2 teaspoons vanilla
1/2 cup water	1 cup whipping cream

Beat together the condensed milk, water, and vanilla. Chill. Beat the whipping cream until thick but not firm. Fold into the condensed milk mixture and pour into a shallow container. Freeze for 1 hour, then stir well. Freeze for at least 2 more hours before serving.

Hurry Up Rhubarb Pudding

Serves 6

1 cup flour	2/3 cup milk
2 teaspoons baking powder	2 cups chopped rhubarb
2 teaspoons sugar	2/3 cup brown sugar
1/8 teaspoon salt	3/4 cup boiling water

Preheat the oven to 375°F and grease a shallow baking dish. In a mixing bowl, sift together the flour, baking powder, white sugar, and salt. Beat in the milk until smooth. Arrange the rhubarb in the prepared baking dish and spread the batter over top. Dissolve the brown sugar in the boiling water, and pour over the batter. Bake for 30 minutes.

St. James Pudding with Hard Sauce

Serves 6–8

This English-style pudding would have been reserved for special occasions such as Christmas. The hard sauce was an extravagance, containing 1/3 cup of butter.

3 tablespoons melted butter	1/4 teaspoon salt
1/2 cup molasses	1/2 pound dried dates or
1/2 cup milk	raisins, chopped
1 1/8 cups flour	**For the Hard Sauce:**
1/4 teaspoon ground nutmeg	1/3 cup butter
1/4 teaspoon ground allspice	1 cup icing sugar
1/4 teaspoon ground cloves	1/2 teaspoon lemon juice
1/2 teaspoon baking soda	1/2 teaspoon vanilla

Beat the melted butter, molasses, and milk until smooth. Sift in the dry ingredients and stir to combine. Fold in the dates or raisins. Pour into a buttered pudding bowl or mould and cover tightly. Set on a rack in a saucepan and pour boiling water to two-thirds of the way up the side of the pudding bowl. Cover and steam for 2 1/2 hours, replenishing the water when necessary. Allow to cool for 20 minutes before turning out onto a serving dish. Meanwhile, make the hard sauce by beating together the ingredients until smooth.

Cranberry Bread Pudding

Serves 6

Waste not, want not—bread puddings put stale bread to tasty use.

2 cups cranberries	3–4 cups coarse breadcrumbs
1 cup water	4 tablespoons melted butter
1 cup sugar	3 tablespoons cream
1 teaspoon cinnamon	

Preheat the oven to 375°F and butter a shallow baking dish. Combine the cranberries, water, and sugar in a saucepan and bring to a simmer. Stir in the cinnamon, cover, and cook for 10 minutes. Toss the breadcrumbs in the butter and put a third of them into the prepared baking dish. Spoon half the cranberries over top. Repeat the layers, ending with the breadcrumbs. Sprinkle the cream over top and bake for 30 minutes. Serve warm.

Chocolate Marshmallow Ice Cream

Serves 6–8

1 1/2 cups condensed milk	16 marshmallows
1/2 cup water	4 tablespoons sugar
2 squares (2 ounces) chocolate, chopped	1/2 teaspoon salt
	1 tablespoon lemon juice

Heat 1/2 cup of condensed milk with the water and chocolate in the top of a double boiler. Stir until the chocolate has melted. Add the marshmallows, sugar, salt, and lemon juice, and continue stirring until the marshmallows have melted and the mixture is smooth. Chill. Beat the remaining cup of evaporated milk until light, and fold into the marshmallow mixture. Pour into a shallow container and freeze for at least 3 hours before serving.

Apple Barley Pudding

Serves 6

This pudding is baked in a warm water bath or "bain-marie," which helps to insulate the dish from the oven's heat. This was a common method for baking custard-style puddings when oven temperatures were less reliable or easy to regulate.

1/3 cup pearl barley	1/4 cup sugar
1/3 teaspoon salt	1 1/2 cups warm milk
4 cups boiling water, lightly salted	1/2 teaspoon vanilla
	2 cups sliced apples
2 eggs, separated	2 tablespoons brown sugar

Preheat the oven to 350°F and lightly grease a baking dish. Place a roasting pan containing a rack and a few inches of water into the oven. On the stove top, cook the barley in the boiling water for 40 minutes, or until most of the water has been absorbed and the grains are tender. Drain. Beat together the egg yolks, sugar, warm milk, and vanilla, and stir into the barley. Whisk the egg whites until firm but not dry, and fold into the batter. Arrange the apple slices in the bottom of the prepared baking dish, and sprinkle with the brown sugar. Cover with the barley mixture. Set the dish on the rack in the roasting pan and cook for 30 minutes, or until the apples are tender. Serve warm.

Hot Cherry Bounce

Serves 8

2 cups flour	**For the sauce:**
3 teaspoons baking powder	1 1/2 tablespoons cornstarch
1/2 teaspoon salt	1 cup cherry juice
1/4 cup quick oats	1/3–1/2 cup sugar
1/4 cup sugar	1 tablespoon butter
1 1/2 teaspoons grated lemon	1 tablespoon lemon juice
zest	1/4 teaspoon almond extract
2 tablespoons butter	1/2 cup canned sour red
1 egg, beaten with 1 cup milk	cherries, pitted
1/2 cup canned sour red	
cherries, pitted	

In a mixing bowl, sift together the flour, baking powder, and salt.
Stir in the oats, sugar, and lemon zest. Cut in the butter. Stir in the
beaten egg and milk just until blended. Fold in the sour cherries and pour
the batter into a greased pudding bowl or mould. Cover tightly. Set on a
rack in a saucepan and pour boiling water to two-thirds of the way up the
side of the pudding bowl. Cover and steam for 45 minutes, replenishing
the water when necessary. Allow to cool for 10 minutes before turning
out onto a serving dish. Meanwhile, combine the cornstarch, cherry juice,
and sugar in a saucepan. Bring to a simmer and cook until thick and
clear, stirring constantly. Stir in the butter, lemon juice, almond extract,
and cherries. Serve hot with the warm pudding.

Cakes, Cookies, and Squares

Despite butter and sugar rationing, and the frequent scarcity and high cost of eggs, wartime housewives prided themselves on serving home-baked goods. As one cookbook author noted: "It will be a sorry day for the small fry when mother doesn't manage to keep the cooky jar filled."

Women gleaned recipes and baking tips from cookbooks such as *250 Ways to Save Sugar*, as well as from newspaper and magazine columns. Honey and molasses were frequently used in place of sugar, eggs were separated and whipped to create volume, and spices or fruit were used to add flavour and moisture to compensate for small measures of fat. Some advice seems unnecessarily complicated, such as this tip for preserving the yolks when a recipe called only for the whites: "Make a hole in both ends of the egg; holding it upright, give it a shake so that the white runs out. Then paste a piece of tape over each hole and the yolks will keep fresh for several days."

Spiced Molasses Cake

Serves 6–8

1 cup molasses	1 teaspoon salt
1 egg	1/2 teaspoon ground cloves
2 1/2 cups flour	1 teaspoon cinnamon
1 teaspoon baking powder	3/4 cup milk
1 teaspoon baking soda	1/2 cup shortening

Preheat the oven to 350°F and grease and flour a 9-inch cake pan. Beat the molasses and egg in a mixing bowl. Sift together the dry ingredients and add to the molasses, alternating with the milk. Mix well, then beat in the shortening until smooth. Pour the batter into the prepared pan and bake for 25–30 minutes, or until a toothpick inserted in the centre comes out clean. Cool for 10 minutes in the pan before turning out onto a rack.

One-Egg Jelly Sponge

Serves 6–8

2 cups flour	1/2 cup corn syrup
2 1/2 teaspoons baking powder	1 egg
	1 teaspoon vanilla
1/4 teaspoon salt	9 tablespoons milk
1/3 cup shortening	1 1/2 cups jelly or jam
1/2 cup sugar	

Preheat the oven to 375°F and grease and flour two 8-inch layer pans. Sift together the flour, baking powder, and salt. In a separate bowl, beat the shortening until creamy and light. Gradually add the sugar and corn syrup, beating until light. Beat in 1 cup of the dry ingredients, followed by the egg and vanilla. Gradually add the remaining flour, alternating with the milk, and stir until smooth. Divide the batter between the pans and bake for 25–30 minutes. Cool for 10 minutes in the pans before turning out onto a rack. When cool, split each layer in two and sandwich all four layers together with jelly or jam.

Economical Fruit Cake

Serves 8

1 cup molasses	1 teaspoon cinnamon
1 egg or 2 yolks	1/2 cup boiling water
1 tablespoon melted butter	1 cup chopped walnuts
2 cups flour	1 cup raisins, soaked in
1 teaspoon baking soda	boiling water and
1/2 teaspoon ground cloves	drained

Preheat the oven to 350°F and grease and flour a loaf pan. Beat together the molasses, egg, and butter. Sift together the dry ingredients and stir into the molasses mixture, alternating with the boiling water. Fold in the nuts and raisins. Pour into the prepared pan and bake for 35–40 minutes, until a toothpick inserted into the centre comes out clean. Cool in the pan.

Honey Cake

Serves 8–10

3/4 cup shortening
3/4 cup honey
3 eggs, beaten
3/4 teaspoon lemon extract
3/4 teaspoon vanilla extract
2 1/4 cups flour
2 1/4 teaspoons baking
  powder

1/4 teaspoon salt
1 cup maraschino cherries,
  chopped
1/2 cup candied peel,
  chopped

Preheat the oven to 325°F and grease and flour a 10 x 10-inch baking pan. In a mixing bowl, cream the shortening until fluffy. Gradually beat in the honey, followed by the eggs, beating well after each addition. Beat in the lemon and vanilla extracts. Sift together the dry ingredients and beat into the shortening and honey mixture. Fold in the cherries and candied peel, and pour into the prepared cake pan. Bake for 1 hour, or until a toothpick inserted into the centre comes out clean. Cool in the pan.

Victory Spice Cake with Prune Filling

Serves 8–10

2 1/4 cups sifted flour
2 1/4 teaspoons baking
    powder
1/4 teaspoon salt
1 1/4 teaspoons cinnamon
1/4 teaspoon ground nutmeg
1/4 teaspoons ground cloves
1/2 cup butter or other
    shortening
1 teaspoon grated lemon zest
1 cup light corn syrup
2 eggs
1 teaspoon vanilla
1/2 cup milk

For the Prune Filling:
1 cup prune juice
3 1/2 tablespoons cornstarch
1/8 teaspoon salt
2 teaspoons lemon juice
3/4 teaspoon grated lemon
    zest
1 teaspoon grated orange zest
2 tablespoons corn syrup
1 cup chopped pitted prunes
1/3 cup chopped nuts

Preheat the oven to 375°F and grease and flour two 8-inch layer pans. Sift together the dry ingredients. In a separate bowl, cream the shortening with the lemon zest. Gradually beat in the corn syrup, until light and fluffy. Add a cup of the dry ingredients and beat until smooth. Add the eggs one at a time, beating well after each addition. Beat in the vanilla and remaining flour, alternating with the milk. Divide the batter between the prepared cake pans and bake for 30 minutes, or until a toothpick inserted in the centre comes out clean. Cool in the pans for 10 minutes before turning out onto a rack.

Meanwhile, heat the prune juice in a saucepan. Mix a little juice with the cornstarch to make a paste, then stir back into the simmering juice with the salt, lemon juice, and citrus zest. Cook gently until thickened, stirring constantly. Add the corn syrup and chopped prunes and mix well. Bring to a simmer and cook for 10–12 minutes, stirring constantly. Remove from heat, stir in the chopped nuts, and allow to cool. Use the filling to sandwich together the cooled cake layers.

Maple Sugar Cake

1 cup maple sugar	**For the frosting:**
1 egg	1/3 cup sugar
1 cup sour cream	3/4 cup maple syrup
2 cups flour	2 egg whites
1 teaspoon baking soda	1/4 teaspoon cream of tartar
1/8 teaspoon salt	pinch salt
1/2 teaspoon cinnamon	

Preheat the oven to 350°F and grease and flour two pie plates. Beat the maple sugar with the egg until smooth and creamy. Beat in the sour cream, then fold in the dry, sifted ingredients. Divide between the prepared pie plates and bake for 25–30 minutes. Cool in the pans. Meanwhile, in the top of a double boiler, combine the sugar, maple syrup, egg whites, cream of tartar and salt. Heat gently while beating constantly for 5-6 minutes, until thick and fluffy. Remove from the heat and cool. Use to frost the cake layers.

Date Crunchies

Makes 3 dozen

1 1/3 cups condensed milk	1 cup pitted dates
1 cup graham cracker crumbs	1 teaspoon cinnamon

Preheat the oven to 375°F and grease a baking sheet. In a mixing bowl, stir together all the ingredients until well blended. Drop by spoonfuls onto the greased baking sheet and bake for 15 minutes.

Molasses Drop Cakes

Makes 3 dozen

3/4 cup molasses	1/2 teaspoon cinnamon
1 egg	1 teaspoon ground ginger
3 cups flour	1/2 teaspoon ground cloves
1/8 teaspoon salt	1 cup sour cream
1/2 teaspoon baking soda	1 cup chopped raisins

Preheat the oven to 325°F and grease a baking sheet. In a mixing bowl, beat the molasses with the egg. Sift together the dry ingredients and add to the molasses, alternating with the sour cream. Beat well. Fold in the raisins. Drop by spoonfuls onto the greased baking sheet. Bake until well browned.

Toastaroons

Makes 40

Commercial breakfast cereals such as Corn Flakes and Puffed Wheat were developed in the early part of the century and gained popularity during the Depression. Wartime bakers soon found good use for these cereals in cookies and squares.

6 cups corn flakes	1 can (14–15 ounces) condensed milk

Preheat the oven to 325°F and grease a baking sheet. Combine the corn flakes and condensed milk, mixing lightly. Drop by teaspoons onto the greased baking sheet, and flatten slightly, shaping the edges with a spoon. Bake for 12–15 minutes. Remove from the baking sheet immediately, using a knife or spatula. If the cookies stick, place the baking sheet over very low heat for a few seconds.

No-Bake Bran and Raisin Drops

Makes 2 1/2 dozen

8 ounces semi-sweet chocolate, chopped	1/2 cup seedless raisins
2/3 cup bran cereal	1/8 teaspoon salt

Melt the chocolate in the top of a double boiler. Combine the cereal, raisins, and salt, and stir into the melted chocolate. Drop by the teaspoonful onto waxed paper and place somewhere cool until hardened.

Cream Cheese Cookies

Makes 2 dozen

3 ounces cream cheese	1 egg yolk, beaten
2 tablespoons butter	1/2 teaspoon vanilla
1/2 cup sugar	1 cup flour

Grease a baking sheet. Beat the cream cheese and butter in a mixing bowl until smooth. Add the sugar, egg yolk, vanilla, and flour. Mix until smooth. Chill. Preheat the oven to 350°F and roll the dough 1/8 inch thick. Use a cookie cutter to stamp out the dough. Bake for 5–10 minutes, until lightly browned.

Gingersnaps

Makes 3 dozen

2/3 cup molasses	2 teaspoons ground ginger
1/3 cup shortening	1/3 teaspoon baking soda
1 3/4 cups flour	3/4 teaspoon salt

Grease a baking sheet. Heat the molasses to boiling, then pour it over the shortening in a bowl. Sift in the dry ingredients and mix well. Chill. Preheat the oven to 350°F and roll the dough 1/8 inch thick. Use a cookie cutter to stamp out the dough. Bake for 8–10 minutes.

Home Front Love Wells

Makes 2 dozen

1/4 cup shortening	1 1/2 teaspoons baking
1/4 cup butter	powder
1/2 cup sugar	1/2 teaspoon salt
2 eggs	tart jelly or jam
2 cups flour	chopped salted nuts

Preheat the oven to 350°F and grease a baking sheet. Cream the fat and sugar in a mixing bowl. Beat in the eggs until blended. Sift half the flour with the baking powder and salt. Stir into the wet ingredients. Continue adding the remaining flour until the dough is just firm enough to roll. Roll out 1/8 inch thick. Use a round cookie cutter to stamp out half the dough. Transfer to the baking sheet. Use a similarly sized doughnut cutter for the remaining dough. Moisten the "doughnut" rings with water and press one on top of each round cookie. Bake for 10 minutes. When cooled, fill centres with jelly or jam, and sprinkle with nuts.

Grape Nut Dainties

Makes 2 dozen

1/2 cup shortening	1/2 teaspoon baking powder
1/4 cup corn syrup	1/8 teaspoon salt
1 egg yolk	Grape Nuts cereal, crushed
1 1/4 cups flour	jelly

Preheat the oven to 300°F and grease a baking sheet. In a mixing bowl, cream the shortening with the corn syrup. Beat in the egg yolk. Sift the flour, baking powder, and salt and stir into the shortening. Shape the mixture into small balls, and dip them into the crushed grape nuts. Transfer to the baking sheet and gently press the centre of each with your thumb. Bake for 5 minutes, remove from the oven, and press the centres down again. Bake 10 minutes longer, remove from the oven, and fill the centres with jam. Allow to cool.

Fudge Nut Squares

Makes 16

7 ounces chocolate chips	1 cup flour
2 tablespoons shortening	1/2 teaspoon baking powder
2 eggs	1/2 teaspoon salt
1/2 cup corn syrup	1/2 cup chopped nuts
1/2 teaspoon vanilla	

Preheat the oven to 375°F and grease an 8-inch square pan. Melt the chocolate and shortening in the top of a double boiler. Remove from heat. In a bowl, beat the eggs well, then beat in the corn syrup and vanilla. Mix until light and fluffy. Stir in the melted chocolate and shortening. Sift together the flour, baking powder, and salt, and stir into the chocolate mixture. Fold in the nuts and pour into the prepared pan. Bake for 25–30 minutes. Allow to cool in the pan before cutting into squares.

Meringue Spice Squares

Makes 16

4 tablespoons fat	1/4 teaspoon ground cloves
1/3 cup brown sugar	1/4 teaspoon cinnamon
1 egg, separated	1/4 cup buttermilk or sour
3/4 cup flour	milk
1/8 teaspoon salt	2 tablespoons sugar
1/4 teaspoon baking soda	2 tablespoons finely chopped
1/4 teaspoon baking powder	nuts

Preheat the oven to 350°F and grease an 8-inch square baking pan. In a bowl, cream the fat and brown sugar until light and fluffy. Beat in the egg yolk. Sift together the flour, salt, baking soda, baking powder and spices, and stir into the creamed mixture, alternating with the buttermilk. Stir until smooth, and pour into the prepared pan. In a clean bowl, whisk the egg white until it holds a peak, and gradually whisk in the sugar until stiff. Spread over the batter and sprinkle the nuts over top. Bake for 25 minutes. Allow to cool in the pan before cutting into squares.

Bread, Muffins, and Biscuits

Although bread was delivered in urban areas by horse and buggy (due to gasoline rationing), many wartime housewives prided themselves on their bread-making skills. Flour was not rationed, and many recipes substituted molasses for sugar and bacon drippings for shortening. Because metal was at a premium during the war, many women baked round loaves in recycled coffee cans.

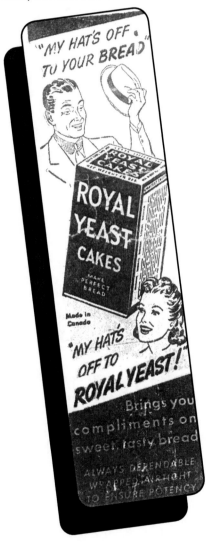

Steamed Brown Bread

Makes 1 loaf

This recipe, submitted to The Halifax Mail *in April 1945 by Mrs. Bernard Mailman of Annapolis Royal, NS, called for "Indian Meal," which we know as fine corn meal. It is a New England recipe in which the bread is steamed rather than baked.*

1 cup flour	1 cup raisins
1 teaspoon salt	1 cup milk
1 cup fine corn meal	1 teaspoon baking soda
1 cup molasses	

Sift together the flour and salt in a bowl. Stir in the corn meal, molasses, and raisins. Add the milk, then dissolve the baking soda in a little hot water and beat it into the mixture. Pour into well-greased coffee cans, cover tightly, and place on a rack in a large pot. Add enough boiling water to the pot to come two-thirds up the sides of the cans. Cover and steam for 2-2 1/2 hours, replenishing the water as necessary. Cool for 10–15 minutes before turning out onto a rack.

Orange Marmalade Biscuits

Makes 12–16

2 cups flour	1 egg
4 teaspoons baking powder	1/3 cup milk
1/2 teaspoon salt	1/3 cup orange marmalade
4 tablespoons shortening	

Preheat the oven to 425°F and grease a baking sheet. Sift together the dry ingredients in a bowl. Cut in the shortening until mixed. Beat the egg with the milk and marmalade and stir into the dry mixture to form a soft dough. Pat out to one-inch thickness, and cut into biscuits. Bake for 10–15 minutes, until browned.

Prize-Winning Bread

Makes 4 large loaves

Even the water used to cook potatoes was put to good use in a well-managed kitchen. The "yeast cakes" that this recipe originally called for are not available at most grocery stores today, but packaged dry yeast works as well and is faster.

1 package active dry yeast	3 cups flour
4 cups potato water	1 tablespoon salt
1/2 cup lard	2–2 1/2 cups warm water
1/3 cup white sugar	

Dissolve the yeast in the potato water. Let stand until foamy, 5–10 minutes. Mix in enough flour to make a sponge. Let rise overnight. In the morning, combine lard, sugar, flour and salt in a saucepan and heat on low until warm. Stir until the ingredients are well blended. Work the sponge into the mixture and add enough warm water to make a pliable dough. Cover and leave until doubled in bulk, about 1 hour. Punch down, shape into four loaves, and set in greased pans. Cover and leave until doubled in size, about 45 minutes. Bake in a preheated 375°F oven for 60–70 minutes, until golden-brown.

Stove-Top Scones

Makes 16

Duncan R. Taylor of Shelburne, NS was surely a Scot, so we'll trust that his recipe works.

4–4 1/2 cups flour	1 teaspoon sugar
1 teaspoon baking powder	1 tablespoon shortening
1 teaspoon salt	1 1/2–2 1/2 cups sour milk
3/4 teaspoon cream of tartar	

Mix together the dry ingredients and cut in the shortening. Stir in enough milk to make a pliable dough. Divide the dough into four parts and roll each into a one-inch-thick round. Cut the round into quarters, and cook in batches on the stovetop in a large, dry frying pan set over medium-low heat. Turn them once they are brown and dry underneath, and continue until they are cooked through.

Molasses Fruit Bread

Makes 1 large loaf

1 cup chopped dried apricots	1 teaspoon cinnamon
1 cup chopped seedless raisins	1/2 cup chopped walnuts
1/2 cup molasses	2 1/2 cups flour
1/4 cup shortening	1 teaspoon baking soda
1 1/2 cups hot water	1/2 teaspoon baking powder
2 teaspoons salt	1 egg, beaten

Combine the apricots, raisins, molasses, shortening, water, salt, and cinnamon in a large pan. Bring to a simmer over low heat, stirring well. Remove from heat and stir in the nuts. Chill. Preheat the oven to 350°F and grease and flour a large loaf pan. Sift together the flour, baking soda, and baking powder. Stir into the chilled mixture along with the beaten egg. Spoon into the prepared loaf pan and bake for 1 hour. Allow to cool in the pan for 10 minutes before turning out onto a rack.

Maple Biscuits

Makes 12–16

2 cups flour	5 tablespoons shortening
1 teaspoon salt	2/3 cup milk
4 teaspoons baking powder	2 cups maple syrup

Preheat the oven to 450°F. Sift together the dry ingredients in a bowl. Cut in the shortening and then stir in the milk. Mix to form a soft dough. Pat out to a 1 inch thickness, and cut into biscuits. Meanwhile, heat the syrup in a saucepan and bring to a boil. Pour the syrup into a baking pan and place the biscuits on top. Bake, uncovered, for 12 minutes.

Oat Muffins

Makes 16

These two wartime muffin tips still hold true: Don't over-mix muffin batter, and grease only the bottom of the muffin cups so that the batter can rise upwards.

1 1/3 cups flour	1/2 cup raisins
1 tablespoon cornstarch	1/2 cup sour milk
2 teaspoons baking powder	1/4 cup cold tea or coffee
1/2 teaspoon baking soda	8 tablespoons melted
2/3 teaspoon salt	shortening
1 teaspoon cinnamon	1 egg yolk, beaten
1 cup quick oats	1/4 cup molasses or corn
1/2 cup brown sugar	syrup

Preheat the oven to 400°F and grease two 8-cup muffin pans. Mix together the dry ingredients in a bowl. Combine the remaining ingredients in a second bowl. Add the dry ingredients to the wet ingredients and stir quickly to combine. Fill the greased muffin cups three-quarters full and bake for 15–20 minutes.

Hot Bacon Muffins

Serve 4–6

1/4 cup butter	5 teaspoons baking powder
2 tablespoons sugar	1 cup milk
1 egg	4 strips of chopped bacon,
2 cups flour	fried until crisp
1/2 teaspoon salt	

Preheat the oven to 350°F and grease an 8-cup muffin pan. Cream the butter and sugar, and beat in the egg. Sift together the dry ingredients and stir into the batter, alternating with the milk. Fold in the bacon. Spoon into the greased muffin cups and bake for 25 minutes. Serve warm.

Apple Muffins

Makes 8

4 tablespoons shortening	1 cup milk
1/2 cup sugar	1 cup finely chopped apples
1 egg, beaten	2 tablespoons sugar
2 1/4 cups flour	1/4 teaspoon ground nutmeg
1/2 teaspoon baking powder	1/4 teaspoon cinnamon
1/2 teaspoon salt	

Preheat the oven to 425°F and grease an 8-cup muffin pan. Cream the shortening and sugar until light and fluffy. Beat in the egg. Sift together the flour, baking powder, and salt, and stir into the creamed mixture, alternating with the milk. Fold in the chopped apples. Spoon into the greased muffin cups and sprinkle the tops with the mixed sugar, nutmeg, and cinnamon. Bake for 20–25 minutes.

Of Course I Can!

Pickles, Relishes, Chutneys, Jams, and Jellies

Of Course I Can!

Along with wartime gardening, every housewife was strongly urged to put up her own preserves in order to conserve as much commercially canned fruits and vegetables as possible for the brave boys at war. Home canning was promoted as yet another means by which women on the home front could participate in the country's war efforts.

A less altruistic incentive for home canning was the additional sugar allowances granted for this purpose. Canning sugar was allowed for all fresh fruits, including citron and wild berries. Marrow, tomatoes, and pumpkins were considered vegetables, and excluded from canning sugar rations. Housewives had to estimate in advance the quantities of sugar they would need for their preserves and complete applications reviewed by the local ration board. Households were then sent special canning sugar coupons, which could be used at specified intervals throughout the harvest months.

The Department of Agriculture recommended canning fruit in preference to making jams and jellies, as plain canning required less sugar and the results were nutritionally more valuable. Women were also instructed not to use canned fruits when fresh fruits were available, and to avoid wasting sugar by careless preparation or storage that resulted in spoilage. On a more sinister note, consumers were warned against the temptations of applying for canning sugar under false pretences. Housewives were required to keep an accurate record of the sugar purchased for canning, and use any excess as part of their regular weekly rations. Not only would "Loyal Canadians be glad of this new opportunity to do their part to ensure Victory," but "False Statements are subject to the Full Penalty of the Law."

Note that many wartime canning recipes substituted molasses for sugar. Molasses adds a rich colour and extra piquancy, particularly to the sweet-and-sour flavour of relishes and chutneys. And because metal was at a premium during the war, women often sealed their jars with melted wax instead of lids. You will have your own preferences.

Pickled Beets

Makes 5 pints

6 cups cooked beets	2 teaspoons mustard seed
4 cups strong vinegar	2 teaspoons celery seed
1 cup molasses	4 teaspoons salt
2 sticks cinnamon	5 small onions, sliced
1 teaspoon whole cloves	

Peel the cooked beets. Leave small beets whole; slice or quarter larger beets. Put remaining ingredients, except for the onions, in a large pot. Bring to a boil and stir until the molasses has melted. Add the beets and onions, and reheat to boiling. Pack the vegetables in hot, sterilized jars. Pour the hot liquid over top and seal jars airtight.

Mustard Pickles

Makes about 5 pints

1 cup coarse salt	6 sweet peppers (red and
4 quarts water	green), seeded and
4 cups large cucumbers, cut	chopped
into pieces	3 cups white sugar
4 cups small cucumbers,	8 cups white vinegar
whole or halved	1/2 tablespoon celery seed
8 cups small whole or	1/2 tablespoon mustard seed
medium-sized sliced	1/4 cup mustard
onions	1 tablespoon turmeric
1 large cauliflower, divided	2/3 cup flour
into florets	

Prepare a brine by dissolving the salt in the water. Pour over the vegetables and leave to soak overnight. Drain. Combine the vinegar and sugar in a large pot and add the celery seed and mustard seed. Bring to a boil. Meanwhile, combine the mustard, turmeric, and flour into a smooth paste with a little vinegar. Stir into the pot. Add the vegetables and bring back to a boil. Remove from heat and pack into hot, sterilized jars. Seal airtight.

Mixed Pickles

Makes about 7 pints

4 quarts ripe tomatoes,
  chopped and drained
2 cups chopped celery
1 cabbage, shredded
2 onions, sliced
2 sweet green peppers, seeded
  and sliced

2 sweet red peppers, seeded
  and sliced
4 cups white sugar
1 cup vinegar
4 tablespoons mustard seed

Mix all the ingredients together in a large pot. Heat slowly, stirring frequently until the sugar dissolves. Pour into hot, sterilized jars and seal airtight.

Vegetable Marrow Chutney

Makes 2 1/2 pints

5 pounds ripe vegetable
  marrow
1 cup salt
3 teaspoons dry mustard
2 teaspoons turmeric
7 1/2 cups malt vinegar
1 teaspoon ground ginger

1/4 cup brown sugar or
  honey
3 sweet red peppers, seeded
  and chopped
1 pound small onions,
  chopped finely

Peel the marrow, cut in half, and scoop out the seeds and stringy flesh. Cut the marrow into small pieces. Cover with the salt and leave overnight. Mix the mustard and turmeric with a little vinegar and add with the remaining vinegar to a large pot. Add the ginger, sugar or honey, peppers and onions, and bring to a boil. Cook for 15 minutes. Drain the marrow and add to the pot. Cook until softened. Pour into hot, sterilized jars and seal airtight.

Mustard Beans

Makes about 7 pints

6 pounds yellow beans,
    chopped in 2-inch
    lengths
3 pints cider vinegar
3 tablespoons brown sugar

1 cup mustard
1 cup flour
2 tablespoons celery seed
1 tablespoon turmeric

Cook the beans in lightly salted boiling water just until tender. Drain. In a large pot, bring the vinegar and sugar to a boil. Combine the mustard, flour, celery seed, and turmeric into a smooth paste with a little of the pot liquid. Stir the mixture into the pot and bring back to a boil. Add the beans and cook 5 minutes. Divide the beans between hot, sterilized jars and pour the pot liquid over top. Seal airtight.

Pickled Onions

Makes about 7 pints

5 pounds small onions,
    peeled
1 cup salt
8 cups white vinegar

1 cup sugar
1/2 cup pickling spices, tied
    in cheesecloth

Sprinkle the onions with salt and leave overnight. Bring the vinegar, sugar, and spices to a boil in a large pot. Rinse and drain the onions and add to the pot. Cook for 5 minutes. Remove and discard the pickling spices. Divide the onions between hot, sterilized jars, and cover them with the pickling liquid. Seal airtight.

Quick Chow Chow

Makes 2 quarts

1 cabbage, cored and
    chopped
2 cups small onions, chopped
2 sweet green peppers, seeded
    and chopped
2 tablespoons salt

4 cups vinegar
1 1/2 cups brown sugar or
    molasses
1/2 cup mustard seed
1 teaspoon celery seed

Combine the vegetables in a large pan and sprinkle with salt. Leave for 1 hour, and then rinse and drain. Bring the vinegar, sugar or molasses, mustard seed and celery seed to a boil in a large pot, and cook for 1 minute. Add the drained vegetables and bring back to the boiling point. Pour into hot, sterilized jars and seal airtight.

Cranberry Relish

Makes about 4 pints

This is a favourite Maritime preserve that we still enjoy, especially at Thanksgiving and Christmas.

3 cups cranberries
3/4 cup vinegar
3 cups brown sugar or
    molasses
flesh and grated zest of
    3 oranges

3 cups seedless raisins
3/4 teaspoon ground cloves
3/4 teaspoon ground
    cinnamon

Cut the cranberries in half and rinse well in a strainer to remove as many seeds as possible. Drain. Bring the vinegar to a boil with the sugar or molasses, orange flesh and zest, and raisins. Add the cranberries and cook for 15 minutes. Stir in the spices and cook 5 minutes more, until thickened. Pour into small, sterilized jars and seal airtight.

Green Tomato Relish

Makes 4 1/2 pints

6 quarts chopped green
    tomatoes
	3 large sweet red peppers,
	    seeded and chopped very
	    finely

5 tablespoons salt	6 large sweet green peppers,
3 cups molasses	seeded and chopped very
4 1/2 cups strong vinegar	finely
1 tablespoon celery seed	1/2 cabbage, cored and
1 tablespoon mustard seed	shredded very finely
1 1/2 teaspoons whole cloves, tied in a bag	3 onions, chopped very finely

Sprinkle the tomatoes with the salt and leave overnight. Rinse and drain. Combine the molasses, vinegar, and spices in a large pot and bring to a boil. Add the vegetables and cook until they are very tender. Remove and discard the cloves and pour the relish into hot, sterilized jars. Seal airtight.

Quick Apple Pepper Relish

Makes 1 pint

1/4 cup lemon juice	1/2 sweet green pepper,
1 cup sugar or molasses	seeded and sliced finely
1/2 teaspoon celery salt	2 large sweet onions, sliced
1/2 teaspoon ground nutmeg	finely
1/2 lemon, sliced finely	3 cooking apples, cored and
1 small can of pimentos, sliced finely	sliced finely

Combine the lemon juice and sugar or molasses in a saucepan and bring to a boil. Stir in the remaining ingredients and bring back to a simmer. Cook, stirring frequently, for 20 minutes. Pour into hot, sterilized jars and seal airtight.

Pickled Orange Slices

Makes about 2 pints

6 oranges	1/2 cup boiling water
cloves	1 teaspoon mustard seed
1 cup sugar	1 stick of cinnamon
1 cup corn syrup	

Cover the oranges with boiling water and cook for 30 minutes. Drain and bring back to the boil with fresh water. Drain again and slice into half-inch-thick segments. Insert a couple of cloves into each slice. Preheat the oven to 375°F. Combine the remaining ingredients in a saucepan and bring to a boil. Cook for 5 minutes, stirring frequently. Arrange the orange slices in a shallow baking dish and pour the syrup over top. Bake for 45 minutes and then transfer to hot, sterilized jars. Seal airtight.

Plum Chutney

Makes about 5 pints

3 pounds plums, stoned and chopped	2 garlic cloves, chopped finely
1/2 pound apples, peeled, cored, and chopped	2 teaspoons salt
1/2 pound raisins	1 teaspoon cayenne pepper
1/2 pound dried currants	1 teaspoon cinnamon
1 1/2 pounds brown sugar or molasses	2 tablespoons grated fresh ginger
2 cups vinegar	2 teaspoons cloves, tied in a bag
juice of 1 lemon	

Combine all the ingredients in a large pot and bring to a boil. Simmer for 2 hours. Remove and discard the cloves and pour the chutney into hot, sterilized jars. Seal airtight.

Strawberry Preserves Two Ways

Method 1:

Select large, firm, tart berries. Rinse and hull. For each pound of fruit use 1 pound of sugar. Combine the berries and sugar in alternate layers in a pot and leave overnight. Heat slowly to boiling, stirring constantly. Boil rapidly for 15–20 minutes, or until the syrup thickens, taking care to prevent it from burning. Remove the surface scum and pour into hot, sterilized jars. Seal airtight.

Method 2:

Pick out the smaller, imperfect berries and crush them in a pot. Heat slowly, stirring constantly, for 3 minutes. Strain the juice back into the pot. Allow 1/4 cup of berry juice and 1 pound of sugar for each pound of whole berries. Add the sugar to the juice, stir, and heat slowly until the sugar has dissolved. Drop the whole berries into the syrup, simmer for 3–5 minutes, then boil rapidly for 10–15 minutes. Remove the surface scum. Leave overnight. Use a slotted spoon to transfer the berries into hot, sterilized jars, filling them three-quarters full. Bring the syrup back to a boil and pour over the berries. Seal jars airtight.

Blueberry Preserves

Makes 4 pints

This recipe was submitted to The Halifax Mail *in April 1945 by Miss Martha Feltmate of White Head, NS. Miss Feltmate claimed that these preserves were grand for making blueberry pies or blueberry duff, a traditional Nova Scotian pudding.*

1 cup sugar	1 cup water
7 cups blueberries	

Combine the sugar and berries in a large pot and stir well. Add the water and bring to a boil. Simmer for 1 1/2 hours, stirring frequently to keep the berries from sticking. Pour into hot, sterilized jars and seal airtight.

Cherry Apple Conserve

Makes 5 pints

3 cups sweet black cherries, pitted	3 cups chopped apples
3 cups sour red cherries, pitted	1/2 cup water
	6 cups sugar

Combine the cherries, apples, and water in a large pot. Bring to a boil and cook for 15 minutes. Stir in the sugar, then drain the fruit and pack into hot, sterilized jars. Seal airtight. The strained juices can be boiled to make a syrup.

Spicy Apple Butter

Makes 6 pints

Given the scarcity of butter for use on toast or waffles, "Spicy Apple Butter" was a popular wartime preserve.

12 pounds tart cooking apples, sliced	1 1/2 teaspoons salt
3 cups hot water	2 teaspoons ground cloves
3 3/4 cups molasses	2 teaspoons ground allspice
1 1/2 cups vinegar	2 tablespoons cinnamon

Combine the sliced apples and water in a large pot and bring to a boil. Cook until the apples have collapsed. Push through a coarse sieve, then return the purée to the pot along with the remaining ingredients. Bring to a simmer and cook for 1 hour, until thickened. Pour into hot, sterilized jars and seal airtight.

Rhubarb and Pineapple Conserve

Makes about 4 pints

4 cups chopped rhubarb
1 can of crushed pineapple
juice and grated zest of
    2 oranges
juice and grated zest of
    1 lemon

1 cup sugar
3/4 cup seedless raisins,
    chopped
1/2 cup chopped walnuts

Combine the rhubarb, pineapple, citrus zest and juices, and sugar in a large pot. Bring to a simmer and cook for 30 minutes. Add the raisins and cook until thickened. Stir in the walnuts and pour into hot, sterilized jars. Seal airtight.

Pear Marmalade

Makes about 7 pints

8 pounds under-ripe pears,
    peeled, cored, and
    chopped
8 pounds sugar
juice and finely chopped rind
    of 3 lemons

1/4 pound fresh ginger,
    peeled and chopped
    finely

Combine the ingredients in a large pot and bring to a boil. Simmer until the pears are tender and translucent, stirring frequently. Transfer to hot, sterilized jars and seal airtight.

Ripe Blackberry Jelly

Makes 3 pints

Blackberries were free for the taking in the countryside, and made a lovely jelly.

2 cups blackberry juice, made
    from 12 quarts ripe
    blackberries
2 cups sugar

2 cups light corn syrup
1 box powdered fruit pectin

Bring the blackberry juice to a boil in a large pot. Stir in the powdered fruit pectin, mix well, and continue stirring until the mixture comes back to a rolling boil. Add the sugar and corn syrup, stirring constantly. Continue stirring and bring back to a rolling boil for 30 seconds. Remove from the heat, skim away any surface scum, and pour into hot, sterilized jars. Seal airtight.

Gooseberry Jam

Makes 4–5 pints

4 cups crushed gooseberries
juice and grated zest of 1
    orange

6 cups sugar

Combine the ingredients in a large pot and let stand 1 hour or more. Bring to a boil. Reduce heat, cover, and simmer for 15 minutes. Remove the lid and bring to a rolling boil, stirring constantly. Boil until thickened. Remove from heat, skim away any surface scum, and pour into hot, sterilized jars. Seal airtight.

In the Spirit of Rationing

Beverages

EFFECTIVE NOW

TEA AND COFFEE

are rationed by coupon

The ration is one ounce of tea **or** four ounces of coffee per person, per week

Coupons A, B, C, D, and E, on the Temporary Wa~~~ Ration Card, now in the hands of the public, are to ~~~ used, and are **NOW** valid for the purchase of tea and coffee.

Each coupon will entitle the purchaser to one ounce tea **or** four ounces of coffee - a supply for one week.

If desired, purchasers may use any or all of these five coupons simultaneously, and buy up to 5 weeks supp~ at one time, on the surrender of the appropriate numb~ of coupons.

Numbered coupons are good only for the purchase sugar and may not be used to buy tea or coffee Similarly, lettered coupons may not be used to buy sugar.

COFFEE CONCENTRATES AND SUBSTITUTES CONTAINING COFFEE

One coupon must be surrendered for each quantity of coffee concentrate or substitute containing coffee, suf- ficient to make 12 cups of beverage.

TEA BAGS REQUIRE COUPONS

When purchasing tea bags, the fol- lowing coupon values shall be used 2 coupons for a carton of 18 or 28 tea 4 coupons for a carton of 48 or 45 tea 8 coupons for a carton of 80 tea bags

CHILDREN UNDER 12 YEARS OF AGE ARE NO~ ELIGIBLE TO RECEIVE ANY RATION OF TEA OR COFF~

SPECIAL NOTICE TO RETAILERS

In the Spirit of Rationing

During the war years, alcohol was increasingly rationed — and scarce. Halifax liquor stores saw block-long queues of men "and an increasing number of women" as alcohol rations continued to decrease. When rationing reached one pint of hard spirits, one quart of wine, or twelve quarts of beer every two weeks, bootleggers' profits soared. In Nova Scotia, professional bootleggers paid up to a dollar over the purchase price to buy spirits from individuals who chose to sell their personal rations rather than drink them. The bootleggers could then re-sell the liquor for as much as 15 dollars a quart, 10 to 15 times more than official Liquor Commission prices.

But teetotallers were affected by rationing as well. In 1942 the Wartime Prices and Trade Board informed consumers that serving tea or coffee at club meetings or garden parties was contrary to the spirit of ration regulations: "ships and sailors' lives must not be put at risk to bring in from abroad a single pound of supplies that we can do without." Individuals over the age of twelve were entitled to either one ounce of tea or four ounces of coffee per week. Parents must have looked forward to their children entering their teens, when they could finally claim caffeine rations. In the meantime, small quantities of coffee or tea could be stretched with milk or juice, and perked up with spices and flavourings—the forerunners of our own favourite coffee-bar drinks.

Spiced Coffee

Serves 8–10

1/2 cup whipping cream	6 cups freshly brewed
1/8 teaspoon cinnamon	coffee
1/8 teaspoon ground nutmeg	cracked ice, to serve

Whip the cream with the spices. Fill each glass halfway with cracked ice, and pour the coffee over top. Serve each glass with a dollop of whipped cream.

Iced Pineapple Coffee

Serves 8

1/4 cup sugar	3 cups cold coffee
3/4 cup water	3/4 cup cream
3/4 teaspoon grated orange	3/4 cup pineapple juice
zest	crushed ice, to serve

Boil the sugar, water and orange zest for 10 minutes. Cool and strain. Stir in the coffee, cream, and pineapple juice. Pour over crushed ice in tall glasses.

Chocolate Syrup

Makes about 1 cup

1 cup water	3 tablespoons cocoa
1/2 cup light corn syrup	

Combine the water, corn syrup, and cocoa in a saucepan. Bring to a simmer and stir frequently for 5 minutes, or until slightly thickened. Keep in a covered jar in the refrigerator until ready to use. Add as needed to hot or cold milk.

Iced Mocha

Serves 6

1/2 cup chocolate syrup
    (see page 99)
2 cups cold milk
1/2 cup cream

1/2 cup strong coffee, chilled
whipped cream and cracked
    ice, to serve

Combine the chocolate syrup, milk, cream, and coffee. Beat or shake well. Pour into glasses half-filled with cracked ice, and top with whipped cream.

Ranchers Coffolate

Serves 8–10

4 cups milk
4 tablespoons finely ground
    coffee
6 cloves
1 cinnamon stick
dash of salt
2 squares (2 ounces) unsweet-
    ened chocolate, chopped

3/4 cup sugar
1 tablespoon flour
1 egg, beaten
cracked ice, to serve

Combine the milk, coffee, cloves, cinnamon stick, and salt in the top of a double boiler. Bring to a boil, then strain. Return the liquid to the pan and stir in the chocolate until melted. Combine the sugar and flour, and stir gradually into the chocolate milk. Cook until thickened, stirring occasionally. Cool slightly and beat in the egg. Chill. Pour over cracked ice in tall glasses.

Grape Tea

Serves 6

3 cups boiling water
3 teaspoons tea leaves
4 tablespoons sugar

2 cups grape juice
juice of 2 lemons

Pour boiling water over the tea leaves. Cover and let stand for 15 minutes. Strain. Stir in the sugar, grape juice, and lemon juice. Chill before serving.

Mulled Pineapple Juice

Serves 4–6

1 cinnamon stick
3 whole cloves
1/4 teaspoon ground allspice
1/4 teaspoon ground nutmeg

4 cups pineapple juice
dash of salt

Tie the spices in a small piece of cheesecloth. Add them to the pineapple juice in a saucepan and bring to a boil. Stir in the salt and serve hot.

Wartime Ginger-Ale

Makes 1 gallon

1 gallon water
1 pint molasses

2 teaspoons ground ginger
cider vinegar

Mix together the water, molasses, and ginger. Stir until combined. Add cider vinegar to taste. Leave for 24 hours before serving very cold.

Sparkling Peach Ice-Cream Soda

Serves 2

1/2 cup mashed ripe peaches
2 scoops of peach or
    chocolate ice-cream

soda water

Divide the peaches and ice-cream between two tall glasses. Mash well and top with soda water. Stir and serve.

Tomato Juice Cocktail

Serves 6

1 large can of tomato juice
1/2 teaspoon celery salt
1 1/2 teaspoons lemon juice
1 1/2 teaspoons vinegar

1/2 teaspoon Worcestershire
    sauce
5 drops Tabasco sauce
cracked ice, to serve

Mix the ingredients thoroughly and serve over cracked ice.

Victory Punch

Serves 12

1 quart vanilla ice-cream,
    softened
1 quart lemon sherbet
1 quart pineapple juice,
    chilled

1 quart ginger ale, chilled
ground nutmeg, to serve

Beat together the ice-cream and sherbet in a large bowl until frothy. Stir in the pineapple juice and ginger ale. Sprinkle each serving with nutmeg.

Index